With love for
Kathy
Colin, Jordan, *and* **Cori**

Donated by Jim Foster

Standing Your Ground

A Call to Courage in an Age of Compromise

Messages from Daniel

ISBN: 0-8010-2538-9

Printed in the United States of America

Contents

Preface

On a mountaintop in Colorado a small gathering of Christians listened to the substance of what follows in this book. Over the course of a week we studied the life of Daniel in the splendor of the Rockies and marveled at the beauty of God's world and his Word. To those who gathered at Horn Creek for those days of rich fellowship I now extend my thanks. Your encouragement lifted me to even greater heights than the peak we climbed and became the inspiration for the work you now hold. In return I pray that you will be encouraged by this reprise of our study. May you face your challenges today strengthened by the testimony of that great servant of conviction named Daniel, whose faith beckons us to climb yet higher mountains for God.

Acknowledgments

The author wishes to express his gratitude to the following:

Covenant Theological Seminary for the opportunity first to deliver these messages and, then, providing the resources and encouragement for the writing of this book.

Mr. Mike Obel for his great aid in helping with the editing of the final manuscript when my own work schedule became so pressing.

Mrs. June Dare for her patient and diligent commitment to seeing the Lord's work done in the production of this book and in her personal walk of faith.

Introduction

Picture the scenario . . . First they take away the children. The best and the brightest of the young are forced to leave their parents and their homeland for "re-education" in a distant land. Next the artists and craftsmen disappear. Not content to plunder the national treasures, the occupation forces herd together ten thousand skilled artisans in one massive deportation campaign and then ship them like prize cattle to the fatherland. There art will be the product of slave labor and the possession of the captors.

Deprived of its young and of its beauty, the captive nation falls into despair, but the worst is yet to come. A nation with its heart rent in two is vulnerable to the cruelest abuses men can conceive. The occupying forces are not content till they have squeezed every drop of gain from the wounded nation. The enemy seizes the crippled country with such a violent shaking that the land is emptied. Not only is the nation looted of its wealth and agriculture, but its people either are killed, must flee to neighboring countries, or are forced to join tens of thousands in a 700-mile death march to slave camps in the enemy capital. In less time than it takes for a child to mature, the occupying army has pillaged an entire nation of its wealth, its people and the heritage of fifteen hundred years.

These atrocities were not the crimes of Hitler or Stalin or the Khmer Rouge. The aggressor was Nebuchadnezzar of Babylon. The victim state was Judah in the time of Daniel. Six hundred years before Christ's birth, Nebuchadnezzar conquered Israel's southern kingdom, and Judah's defeat was the final blow to the glory days of the Israelites' history. The northern kingdom had already fallen to Assyria over a century earlier. The days of Saul, David, and Solomon were long past. Wicked kings and sinful passions had ruled and divided Israel for most of the preceding 350 years. Weakened by sin, division, and decadence, its people were no match for the onslaught of Nebuchadnezzar, the pagan king whose conquest was brutal and whose rule was savage. Only by comparing Nebuchadnezzar's ruthless actions with the worst terrors of this century can we see beyond the pictures in Sunday school quarterlies to comprehend the actual cruelty he dispensed. He stole Judah's wealth, robbed her of hope through three massive campaigns of exile and enslavement, and almost completely destroyed her heritage by driving the people from the land and demolishing every vestige of culture that might lure them back. In 586 B.C. Nebuchadnezzar razed the temple and leveled the city of Jerusalem.

Onto this stage of ruin walked Daniel. He was one of the youths that Nebuchadnezzar stole from Judah in the first wave of exile. We know little about Daniel's life prior to the time that he was brought as a captive to train for the king's service. What we do know is that his situation seemed hopeless. He was nearly a thousand miles from home. His land was shattered. His family and friends were scattered or in captivity. His people had abandoned their God, so it was only natural in this punishing state of exile to believe that God had abandoned his people. But Daniel never believed what merely "seemed" to be true. He believed what God said, and God had promised that he would never forsake his people. Although they might become faithless, he would remain faithful to his Word. Because Daniel believed in this faithful God, he resolved to stand for the Lord, even in the midst of Babylon's wickedness and his own people's weaknesses. Time after time Daniel was tempted to abandon his God—often with his own life at stake. Each time Daniel stood his ground.

The first six chapters of the Book of Daniel, upon which

this book focuses, are the history of the prophet's stand. The accounts of these chapters span Daniel's life from early adulthood to advanced age. As diverse as the stories are, one thread ties the biography together: Daniel's faithfulness to God despite the pressures and threats of those about him. Daniel was never too old nor too young to escape severe temptations to compromise his spiritual integrity, but—despite constant cultural pressures—Daniel refused to yield. As a result, Daniel's life story is a rich resource for believers in any culture who face intense pressures to compromise their commitments to God.

You may be a believer facing similar assaults on your faith life. The pressures may come from job requirements, the expectations of friends, family tensions, or your doubts that God is truly present in your life. If you know these faith trials, this book is for you. Daniel's biography not only confirms the integrity of the man who penned the subsequent prophecies, it reveals how any of God's people may yet find the grace to stand when their world is collapsing.

Daniel's history reminds Christians under pressure that God's work is not done till he has won. Although temptations are severe, and trials seem overwhelming, God will overcome apparently impossible odds through those who stand firm in the power of his might. In Daniel's story, God says that faithfulness will be victorious. God will accomplish his purpose. His compassion will not fail. His plan is never off schedule. Delay does not signal defeat, any more than disaster reveals godly indifference or divine weakness. The sovereign God saves as only *he* knows is best, using those who remain true to him. Patient confidence in God's ultimate good is never mistaken. God will work through courageous faithfulness. All you must do is stand your ground!

1

The Undefiled

(Daniel 1)

The Word

I walked into our kitchen just as my wife threw away an entire gallon of newly purchased milk. She turned the jug upside down over the sink. With a gasping "glug, glug, glug," the plastic container coughed out its contents in seconds. Kathy waved a hand in my direction to reassure me she hadn't lost her marbles with the milk. "The safety seal was broken," she said. Then I understood. She had opened the lid to serve our child, and there it stared up at her—the broken safety seal. Probably she had hesitated a moment, thinking about the waste of money and the minuscule likelihood that something really was wrong with the milk. Then she remembered the news reports of foods tainted and medicine poisoned by lunatic tampering. She remembered why the safety seal was on the milk. A glance at the precious face of our child suddenly made the risk, however slight, too great. The milk went down the drain. What was being protected was of infinitely greater value.

Daniel and his three friends faced similar concerns. These four young captives in a foreign land refused the royal food because they, too, feared their food was contaminated. This contamination, however, did not threaten their bodies, their physical well-being. The four faced a far more potent pollutant, for the food they refused could poison their souls. The lethal ingredients threatened their holiness. To avoid such contamination was not without potential costs in this cruel land. The first chapter of Daniel makes it clear that certain personal risks may accompany one's commitment to holiness. But God makes it just as plain in this part of his Word that the price tag of holiness cannot be compared with the infinitely greater value of what is being protected.

1In the third year of the reign of Jehoiakim king of Judah,
Nebuchadnezzar king of Babylon came to Jerusalem and
besieged it. 2And the Lord delivered Jehoiakim king of Judah
into his hand, along with some of the articles from the temple
of God. These he carried off to the temple of his god in Bab-
ylonia and put in the treasure house of his god.

3Then the king ordered Ashpenaz, chief of his court offi-
cials, to bring in some of the Israelites from the royal family
and the nobility—4young men without any physical defect,
handsome, showing aptitude for every kind of learning, well
informed, quick to understand, and qualified to serve in the
king's palace. He was to teach them the language and litera-
ture of the Babylonians. 5The king assigned them a daily
amount of food and wine from the king's table. They were to
be trained for three years, and after that they were to enter
the king's service.

6Among these were some from Judah: Daniel, Hananiah,
Mishael and Azariah. 7The chief official gave them new
names: to Daniel, the name Belteshazzar; to Hananiah, Shad-
rach; to Mishael, Meshach; and to Azariah, Abednego.

8***But Daniel resolved not to defile himself with the royal
food and wine, and he asked the chief official for permis-
sion not to defile himself this way.*** 9Now God had caused
the official to show favor and sympathy to Daniel, 10but the
official told Daniel, "I am afraid of my lord the king, who has
assigned your food and drink. Why should he see you looking
worse than the other young men your age? The king would
then have my head because of you."

11Daniel then said to the guard whom the chief official had
appointed over Daniel, Hananiah, Mishael and Azariah,
12"Please test your servants for ten days: Give us nothing but
vegetables to eat and water to drink. 13Then compare our

appearance with that of the young men who eat the royal food,
and treat your servants in accordance with what you see."
[14]So he agreed to this and tested them for ten days.
[15]***At the end of the ten days they looked healthier and***
better nourished than any of the young men who ate the
royal food. [16]So the guard took away their choice food and
the wine they were to drink and gave them vegetables instead.
[17]***To these four young men God gave knowledge and***
understanding of all kinds of literature and learning. And
Daniel could understand visions and dreams of all kinds.
[18]At the end of the time set by the king to bring them in,
the chief official presented them to Nebuchadnezzar. [19]The
king talked with them, and he found none equal to Daniel,
Hananiah, Mishael and Azariah; so they entered the king's
service. [20]In every matter of wisdom and understanding about
which the king questioned them, he found them ten times
better than all the magicians and enchanters in his whole
kingdom.
[21]And Daniel remained there until the first year of King
Cyrus.

Daniel 1 (*Emphasis added*)

Karen's Predicament

The lunatic poisoning of retail medicines and foods has made product contamination a common and justifiable concern today. But concern over another form of contamination was even more critical for two friends of mine: Randy, a full-time seminary student, and his wife, Karen. Like the wives of many seminarians, Karen was earning money to keep her husband in school and food on the table. In her case, Karen earned money as a quality-control inspector for a major pharmaceutical company.

One day, through faulty procedures, the automated machines produced a large order of syringes that became contaminated and therefore failed inspection. Karen reported the problem to her boss, but he quickly computed the costs of reproducing the order and made a "cost-effective" decision. Because so much money would be lost in reproducing the syringes, the boss ordered Karen to sign the inspection clearance despite the contamination. Although she refused, this did not get her off the hook.

Because of certain federal regulations, only Karen could sign the clearance forms. If Karen did not sign, the syringes could not be marketed. The boss urged and threatened, but Karen would not budge. The impasse between Karen and her superior led to a visit from the company president. He also computed the costs of reproduction and issued his decision: the forms must be signed. Karen would have the weekend to think over whether or not she would sign the clearances. On Monday, the president said that if Karen was still determined not to sign the forms, her job would be in jeopardy.

In fact, much more than Karen's job was in jeopardy. Because her inspection job was this couple's only means of support, Randy's education and their family's future were severely endangered. The hopes, dreams, and career plans of many years could be shattered as a result of a choice to be made in only two days. For this young couple, all the theological jargon and doctrinal instruction about consecration, righteousness, and holiness suddenly came down to this one concrete decision: could they afford to remain undefiled from the contamination the world of business practicalities urged Karen to approve?

This couple's predicament was similar to what God's people have faced in all ages. The first chapter of Daniel well illustrates that there have always been pressures on believers to pollute the purity of their dedication to God. Because this pattern of pressure is so consistent, we should never naively believe there are no spiritual contaminants around *us* to poison minds and hearts and defile our relationship with the Lord. Finances, employers, friends, relatives, or our own desires make demands. The pressures confront anyone who seeks to live uncompromisingly for Christ. Since God still calls his people to be faithful to him, if we are to live undefiled before the world, we must gauge the risks, reasons, and rewards of holiness.

The Risks of Holiness

Too often Christians do not stand up for the Lord because more mature believers have not spoken plainly about the risks of holiness and prepared them for the price to be paid. If we are to live for the Lord without being defiled by what the world urges us to approve, we must first count these risks. This is just a matter of playing "heads-up baseball." You cannot perform your duties or hold your position if you do not know what might come your way. Daniel makes us aware of the difficult plays that may be hit in our direction if we seek to stand our ground for the Lord.

The facts of Daniel's life are simple enough. He was a prisoner of war in Babylon. He had come from a noble family, but Babylon's conquest, deportation, and captivity of the people of Judah apparently dimmed any hope of power or honor Daniel might have had. Although his future once looked bright, it now lay in shadows. Then came an unexpected opportunity. King Nebuchadnezzar of Babylon wanted some young Israelites trained for government service, probably to manage their captive compatriots. As a result, Daniel and other promising young Jewish slaves began training for positions of honor and power. All Daniel needed to do was go along and accept the privileges others were enjoying—and a future once blighted would shine again. To question any of the privileges might jeopardize not only Daniel's future but his life as well.

But Daniel *did* question. For reasons that are not entirely clear (but probably focused on the "unclean" meat and wine used in Babylonian idolatry), Daniel believed he would defile himself if he ate and drank what was served to him. The Bible records that "Daniel resolved not to defile himself with the royal food and wine, and he asked the chief official for permission not to defile himself this way" (Dan. 1:8). Instead, he requested only vegetables and water for himself and his friends.

These facts are so familiar and so bathed in the aura of Sunday-school storytime that we may miss the great risk Daniel took in resolving not to defile himself. Imagine an eighteen-year-old young man today. Although he is handsome, talented, intelligent, and shows great promise, he cannot afford college because his family is poor. He graduates from high school, only to spend one miserable day after another flipping hamburgers at the local Burger Palace. Then, out of the blue, something amazing happens. He comes home one day, sweating and smelling of french fries, and his mother meets him at the door.

"The president is on the phone for you," she says.

"Sure, Mom," he says. "That really cheers me up."

"No, honey," she says, "I mean it. The president of the United States is on the phone—for you."

It is true! The president is on the phone. "Son," he says, "I hear you have all the smarts and talent in the world but just haven't gotten an even break. I'm going to make it up to you."

The young man nearly faints as he listens to the president's offer: a full scholarship to an excellent university near Washington, D.C. The president says the young man can live in the White House, eat with him, and even get a Secret Service escort to and from school. Further, upon graduation the young man will be awarded an ambassador's position in the diplomatic service. The young man with such promise has been living in poverty and obscurity, but suddenly he is going to have all the world can offer. His potential will be realized, his dreams fulfilled.

One slight hitch. The president says that because the young man is being groomed for a job in the State Department he should begin practicing diplomacy now.

"We hear," says the president, "that you're a committed

Christian. That's great. A little religion is good for anyone. However, we get a lot of different people from different places and religions coming through the White House. We don't want to embarrass or upset anyone. So I want a promise from you that you will never attend church as long as you live in my house or work in the foreign service."

If you can picture yourself as that young person, what would you say? Would you make that promise? Would you, in like circumstances, risk such a rosy future and pay the price to remain undefiled?

Removed from the actual situation and the pressures of reality, we might find it easy to say we *would* risk security and success for holiness. But is it that simple? If your wife were being asked to sign a clearance form for contaminated products and her decision determined the future of your career and family plans, would the choice be cut-and-dried? Regardless of what you might like to think, a commitment to holiness is never easy. The risks of holiness are very real, and they are always present. By the way, Karen *did* refuse to sign the clearance forms for the contaminated syringes. And it cost her the job.

Never minimize the risks of holiness. Never pretend that living for the Lord is painless, easy, or always fun—for then you are abandoning and abusing those who have suffered for their stand. Whenever we pretend that holiness is easy, we fail to prepare those who must take a stand in this world. And the time will come for every believer when such a stand must be made. We, too, have idolatries in our culture that demand obedience and produce defilement. The idols we are prone to serve today are success, security, and pleasure. They may not sound sinister, but their spiritual effects can be just as defiling as Nebuchadnezzar's feasts.

Many Christians all around us feel deeply compromised by what they do on the job every day for income, seniority, and position. Whether because of the products they make, services they render, or unethical decisions they execute, they are conscience-stricken. But they do not know what to do! The fear about job loss keeps them saying, "I'm sorry the boss is out of the office," when he is not. Fear about loss of pensions keeps them on the job producing and marketing products abhorrent to God. Fear about loss of profit perpetuates such business lies as "The check is in the mail," and "We'll get on it first thing tomorrow." Fear about loss of prestige and status keeps us excusing our immoral actions by saying, "I've done it so long that they would laugh if I said no now." Fear about tomorrow's uncertainties or loss of a comfortable lifestyle makes us all rationalize at times that "I have no choice. I cannot afford the risk." Reasons may vary, but results are often the same: holiness is deemed "too risky." The upshot is believers whose spiritual lives are crumbling because their jobs are eating away at their souls.

What will ease such a Christian's conscience and still his or her heart's anguish? *Holiness*. But never the kind of nominal holiness that fails to speak plainly of the risks it brings. We believers must recognize what will happen to us if we really stand for our God in every circumstance. We may suffer, true, but holiness is not a matter of minimizing these consequences but of preparing for them. If we have not been honest about the risks of holiness, they will seem unusual, atypical, or extraordinary when they appear. If a trial is seen as exceptional, it will also be viewed as somehow unfair or unnecessary because others do not appear to face the same battles. But no battle is "unfair" for an individual believer who has recognized that the risks are real for all who will stand for holiness.

There is a communion or fellowship of risk that enfolds all who strive for holiness. We will each be more willing to stand for the Lord and less prone to fall into discouragement when we are aware of the risks we share with faithful believers like Karen and Daniel. Conversely, it is a cruel dishonesty not to identify the risks of holiness, for then believers doubt themselves during times of struggle—as though there is something wrong with them alone.

The fellowship that enfolds each one who takes risks to

be holy even includes "the author and perfecter of our faith" (Heb. 12:2). From a bloodstained cross on a hill called Golgotha, the Lord made clear to all the risks of holiness. Even complete holiness does not guarantee this world's rewards. The world may readily praise idealism, but it rarely tolerates ideals. The world did not, could not, understand Jesus Christ. Why, then, should we expect the world to understand us if we stand for him, or be surprised if our experience with the world duplicates his on a smaller scale? Holiness necessitates risk for us. Jesus' suffering, of course, was a certainty! He knew the world would not accept him, and still he came from glory and died for sinners like you and me. Now, for Christ's sake, we must resolve not to defile ourselves. Jesus is our model and our motivation for holiness. Because he offered his life for us, we must yield our lives to him for his purposes. We cite the risks of holiness only to avoid being deterred by fear of those consequences. We acknowledge the risks so we may aspire to holiness as an informed choice.

The Reasons for Holiness

Despite an initial willingness to assume risks, we may still falter in staying faithful if we see no practical reason for the holiness to which God calls us. We can take many blows and bear heavy burdens if the purpose is clear. God knows this about us and uses Daniel's life to explain *why* we must stand firm for the Lord in difficult situations.

Preparation

The first reason for holiness in this early trial of Daniel's life is that his stand prepared him for spiritual battles ahead. Starting with this first chapter, the Book of Daniel goes from one cliff-hanging, spine-tingling adventure to the next. A quick scan of the next five chapters finds Daniel and his friends facing death-dealing kings, dazzling dreams, a golden idol, a fiery furnace, a king turned into an animal, a palace plot, and a lions' den. Steven Spielberg would love this material. Each trial leads to a new and greater challenge—and that is just the point. Daniel's temptation to defile himself never ceased. Contamination keeps on threatening lives kept pure for God. The purpose revealed in Daniel's initial choice of holiness was preparation for battles lying ahead.

The truth that today's holiness is preparation for tomorrow's battles sounds simple enough, but it is a truth Christians often ignore. We play games in our minds and say, "If the Nazis dragged me from my home and threatened to machine-gun me if I would not deny my faith, I would stand firm." Or "If Attila the Hun tied me to a stake and said, 'Recant or die,' I would never deny Jesus." We imagine that if the day ever came when we really had to stand firm for holiness, we would offer our lives for the faith. As we dream about standing firm in that "someday," we often let the little things slide in the meantime! We seem less willing to offer our lives in the little battles for honesty, integrity, and chastity that rage about us in ordinary situations. And it is the loss of those minor skirmishes that cripples today's walk of faith.

In the eighteenth century, the Holy Spirit blessed the United States with a widespread revival that came to be known as the Great Awakening. One of the means God used to prepare for and then fuel this revival was a renewed holiness among pastors and evangelists. A young Presbyterian minister named Gilbert Tennant sparked this spiritual awakening with an influential sermon entitled "The Dangers of an Unconverted Ministry." Tennant identified the great threat that always endangers the church when hypocrisy and compromise infect the very ones whose holiness ought to be exemplary. That threat to holiness two centuries ago was no greater than it is today. As unholy entertainments, selfish lifestyles, and an increasingly secularized society encroach more and more on the people of God, holiness has never seemed of less practical value, nor has it ever been more threatened.

It grieves me to think about the number of my peers in ministry who are no longer pastors because of moral lapses. Even more have confided, "Bryan, I came so close, too." And I am not recounting the accumulated toll of many years. As a young minister, it scares me to see how quickly so many have fallen and to recognize that more will fall in the future. I am not condemning these men. Many are my friends. You may know such men and love them as I do. They are mentioned not to hurt anyone but so that we may learn from their examples. We are all capable of stumbling. If the world has so touched the leaders of the church, we can be sure that others among the people of God have not remained unscathed.

It is increasingly apparent that the moral lapses of these leaders sprang from hearts not uncompromisingly committed to holiness. Sin will easily snare hearts accustomed to dabbling on the fringes of biblical license and Christian liberty in their entertainments, personal ethics, and relationships. Seemingly innocuous compromises—choices no one condemns for fear of appearing prudish or legalistic—can produce devastating sin in the lives of sincere believers. We must be aware of this pathology of sin sickness because we are all vulnerable.

Just as the Christian church in the eighteenth century benefited from a renewed commitment to holiness, so the church today cannot flourish until we heed the great threat to holiness that Gilbert Tennant identified so long ago. The effects of moral illness among some of our most visible leaders today has been much in the news, but the fact that God's people did not recognize the warning signs before the collapses made headlines indicates that the illness has not affected merely the "head" of the religious establishment. The body, too, is sick. Contamination threatens us all if we do not prepare to withstand its continuous assault.

Through Daniel's early life, God teaches us that holiness, like most Christian graces, does not spring fully developed into the believer's heart, and that heart cannot bear the load for which it has not prepared. Daily we must seek Christ's strength and intervention in our lives. If we are not dedicated to holiness today, we will not be undefiled tomorrow. Each day of holiness is training for tomorrow's conflicts. If we walk away from Jesus on today's training ground, it will not be easy to find him on tomorrow's field of battle.

Protection

God's further purpose in our holiness is to shield us from spiritual harm. Today's holiness not only prepares us for tomorrow's battles, but protects us from the devastating effects of the enemy's victories.

During my summers as a college student, I worked for a major road-construction company in western Tennessee. As an assistant to one of the supervisors, I earned excellent pay. That was important because the university I attended was very expensive, and neither I nor my family had the money to pay for my education. Jobs were hard to come by, so it was vital to my future that I hold this one.

One morning my supervisor told me I was doing such a good job for him and the company that he was going to give me a special privilege. He owned a hunting lodge in a nearby county, and he wanted me to spend a day or two there enjoying the outdoors. I thanked him for the offer but explained I needed every day of work I could get for college expenses and could not afford the time off.

"Don't worry about that," he said. "You just do a little painting and repair at my cabin while you're there, and I'll keep you on the payroll."

I was off like a shot. By that evening I was at the cabin, savoring a meal of fresh catfish and looking forward to a day of uninterrupted ease. Then the telephone rang. It was my father calling. When he had gotten home from work that evening, my mother had explained where I was and under what arrangements. Dad phoned me right away.

"What are you doing collecting company pay for private work?" he asked.

Well, I had not quite thought of it that way. I did not want to think of it that way.

"Dad," I said, "I can't go back to my boss now and tell him what he asked me to do is unethical. He may get offended, and I may lose this job. How am I going to get through school if I don't have this job?"

Dad replied, "I know you need this job to prepare for what you want to do. I also know what you need to prepare for life—and this is not it."

I went home. I knew he was right. And, as I have gotten further from the situation, I have understood even more how right he was. My father accurately saw that one careless action could lead to further compromises and greater harm. If the deceit, however slight it seemed, had worked that time, what kind of precedent would it have established in my life? Would I have looked back at some point on a successful career and said, "Look how beneficial it was for me to be unethical at that point"? If so, what decisions might I be tempted to make at difficult moments in that career? What greater danger might I place myself in by believing that past compromise had helped me?

One reason why careless defilement of holy commitments cannot be permitted is that it only leads to further wrong and harm. If we do not practice holiness today, it will not protect us tomorrow. The consequences of sin are pleasant only for a season, then the result is great and lasting hurt. God protects us from this future hurt by calling us to present holiness. Our challenge is to make this present commitment. Because of pressures and difficulties, some of you may have said recently, "I will serve the Lord better, but *later.*" Forgive me if this sounds too harsh, but no, you will not! If you are not preparing for tomorrow with holiness today, you will not be able to stand for the Lord later. Today's battles are preparation and protection for tomorrow's assaults. *Now* is the time to be undefiled. *Later* will be too late.

The Rewards of Holiness

The preparation and protection afforded by holiness indicate that God's commands for purity are neither arbitrary nor capricious. The Bible's call to holiness reflects the Author's goodness and love for us, his children. God's love indicates that holiness is never meant to be a burden. On the contrary, holiness brings many rewards. As we see these rewards in Daniel's life, we are more willing and able to serve God without defilement.

Witness

The first reward of holiness that beacons in this first chapter of Daniel is evident in the effect of his witness. Daniel's testimony—his stand for holiness—affected others. Daniel became a light to others, leading them from temptation and to God. Daniel resolved not to defile himself by eating the royal food, and Shadrach, Meshach, and Abednego joined the cause (1:8, 11–12). This was a critical moment in the lives of Daniel's three friends because soon they would have to stand alone in a blazing furnace (see chapter 3). Daniel's witness prepared Shadrach, Meshach, and Abednego to become witnesses, too.

But Daniel's witness did not affect only his friends. The names of two pagan kings, Nebuchadnezzar and Cyrus, appear in this first chapter of the Book of Daniel (vv. 1, 21). The introduction of these kings frames the chapter, and their lives were to frame Daniel's ministry. As later chapters reveal, Daniel's witness had an amazing effect on these two men. They, in turn, changed history. And it all began when Daniel decided to dine on vegetables and water rather than steak and wine. That spark of witness became a beacon of holiness that changed innumerable lives for eternity.

If you are like most committed believers, however, your deepest yearning is not so much to see God change "innumerable lives" for eternity as it is to see him change a particular life. There is probably not one of us committed to the Lord Jesus who does not long to see a certain family member or friend brought to the Lord. Most of us would give everything we have if it would bring that person to a saving knowledge of Jesus Christ, and we have prayed and prayed and prayed for God to bring that to pass. God tells us through Daniel that holiness reaches hearts. We may have shared our testimony a thousand times. We may have mouthed a thousand prayers. But ultimately we must ask ourselves whether we have really witnessed with holy lives—our own. Are our lives undefiled before those watching eyes? Have we taken a stand for holiness in the small things as well as the great? There is no greater joy and no greater reward for a believer than to see God use one's holiness to make another heart his own. And there is no more powerful witness than an undefiled life.

In the small denomination I serve there is one family that has produced outstanding Christian leaders for two generations. Some of our most notable and effective pastors, missionaries, and lay leaders come from this one extended family. The making of these brightly shining Christian beacons was no chance occurrence. Three generations ago the matriarch of this brood of witnesses accepted Jesus as her Lord and Savior, though her husband did not. Eleven children were born to the couple. As a Christian mother and wife, this woman remained faithful in her holiness for a lifetime. She gave careful Bible instruction to her children and was conscientious in her love and prayers for her husband. Each of the children became a believer and a church leader. Each child raised a family of believers and church leaders. Meanwhile, all the children continued to pray for their father. After two generations, thousands of lives have been nurtured, changed, and won for Jesus because of the reverberating impact of this one woman's faithful witness. That might be reward enough, but God was not done. After decades of prayer and a life of witness, the original beacon of holiness saw the light of faith in her husband's eyes, too. As he received Jesus as his Lord and Savior, here was abundant reward "pressed down, shaken together and running over" (Luke 6:38).

Welfare

Besides the reward of being a shining witness, this first chapter of Daniel indicates another blessing that accompanies holiness. God not only used Daniel's witness; he made provision for that witness to continue until it accomplished all he intended. God provided for Daniel's personal welfare. Daniel's physical needs were supplied amply, though he appears to have been "disadvantaged" from a worldly point of view. Even without the lavish royal food, Daniel's health prospered (1:15). Even though great risks were taken, Daniel's life was preserved. He and the others were given "knowledge and understanding" (v. 17). As a matter of fact, before Daniel completed his life's service, kings and kingdoms would come and go, but the Lord kept Daniel safe. God is always concerned for the personal welfare of his holy witnesses.

Remember Karen, forced to leave her job at the pharmaceutical company? God did not abandon her. Because she would not sign the clearance forms for the contaminated syringes, the order was not delivered to the customer on time. Officials of that company investigated the delay and discovered how Karen had protected them from the contaminated syringes, even at the cost of her own job. The customer then hired Karen and increased her pay. Karen finished putting Randy through seminary and now serves with him as he pastors a thriving church in New Mexico. (I also experienced something similar with my road-crew supervisor. When I followed my father's advice and told my boss I could not do private work for company pay, he simply said, "Okay" and did not fire me.)

These "success stories," whether of characters biblical or contemporary, might be somewhat misleading, simply because they turn out nice and neat. Of course, life does not always come packaged with so pretty a ribbon tied around it. Some of us may receive few if any tangible rewards for our holiness till we are in heaven with the Lord. Till that time, some may never see the fruits of resisting defilement. But what the lives of Daniel and Karen make clear is that God does not abandon his own. ". . . he rewards those who earnestly seek him" (Heb. 11:6). The rewards, whether earthly or heavenly, are guaranteed. God always safeguards the personal welfare of his witnesses in the way he knows is best. We can always afford the price of serving God, because the real risks of holiness never outweigh the inevitable rewards.

Although there are not always tangible benefits (with negligible damages) as a result of holiness, this life is only a moment in God's time (see Psalm 90). Our immediate concerns are almost nothing compared to the immense concerns God has for our souls. The rewards of holiness are often introduced in the present, but they are intended for an eternity (see John 14:2; Rev. 21:4). Because God safeguards the personal welfare of his own with a view to what provides for their *ultimate* good and the good of the lives they touch (see 2 Tim. 4:6–8, 16–18), Daniel's circumstances remained dire in many ways. He was still a captive in a pagan land, with many more trials and tragedies to face. Yet God safeguarded and guided Daniel in a way that even the worst-seeming disasters became instruments of God's grace for him and others. A holy person is a powerful tool in God's hands. Although God may use the tool for difficult tasks, he will cherish the tool and always use it with great care. As we pursue holiness, our welfare is God's delight.

God preserved Daniel's physical health after his decision to avoid defilement, but there was more to God's reward than mere bodily well-being. Something also happened to Daniel and his friends internally as a result of their holiness. They entered into so close a relationship with God that his indwelling Spirit empowered them to do acts beyond their own ability. Daniel and his friends shared a greater wisdom than their Jewish peers and Babylonian teachers (1:20). Daniel could even "understand visions and dreams of all kinds" (v. 17). Many more trials and dangers would face Daniel and his friends, but God had prepared them inwardly to meet those challenges. Without such internal strengthening, our spiritual and emotional lives would crumble.

When I was in the sixth grade, my father brought home a fifty-pound sack of walnuts from his parents' farm. These walnuts were not like the ones you buy at a grocery store. Walnuts sold at a grocery store have already been processed. They still may have a shell, but usually someone has removed the thick, tough husk that coats the walnuts while they are on the tree. Store-bought walnuts are only about the size of a golf ball. Walnuts still in the husk approach the size of a tennis ball.

Although getting those husks off the walnuts can be quite a chore, my father had a solution he learned on the farm. Sometimes farmers simply scatter the nuts in their husks over a gravel driveway. Fresh walnut shells can withstand the weight of a vehicle in the loose rock, but the repeated crunching between tires and gravel eventually rubs off the husks. Since this process had the imprimatur of tradition, with some ceremony my dad spread the walnuts on our gravel driveway. All seemed fine until the first set of car tires squeezed over the batch of walnuts. Moisture or some insect had penetrated those walnuts and destroyed their insides. They looked fine on the outside, but when the pressure of the car's weight rolled over the shells, each one cracked and revealed a black smelly mess within. The contamination inside destroyed their ability to stand up to the outside pressure.

God is concerned for the holiness of each of us because he knows the pressures that will come. Because their hearts are one with the Lord, some will be able to withstand the pressures that challenge their faith. God's strength and courage will bolster and sustain them. Others, perhaps someone reading this book at this moment, recognize that such pressures would reveal a heart that is dark and defiled. If, because of unholiness, God's strength and sustenance are not inside a person, the pressures that surely will come have the potential to crack the best-preserved exterior.

Why speak of human lives as "cracked shells"? Are you a Humpty Dumpty who—once cracked—cannot be put back together again? No! Daniel did not see the future and stand for God because of his own independent ability. This youth's understanding of dreams and prophecies was the result of God's working in him. The same God can work in you. He is the God who says that, though your heart be dark as coal, he can make it white as snow. If your heart is broken, ruined, and defiled by unholiness, recognize the One who alone can make you whole and clean again. God does not expect us to be holy apart from him. God sets the standard of holiness, but he also provides the means of holiness as we confess our sin to him and come to him for his cleansing through Jesus Christ. Our understanding of what God does for our spiritual welfare both tells us the true source of holiness and motivates us to seek it more.

Motivation for Holiness

Yes, the risks of holiness are great. All of us would at times rather run from holiness than embrace it. But God uses personal holiness to prepare us for the spiritual enemies we will face. There are reasons that make sense of the risks. More than that, there are rewards that make the risks not really risks at all. God has the personal welfare of his holy instruments at heart and will use our holiness to change the hearts of loved ones and make our own hearts whole again. When we see clearly the risks, reasons, and rewards of holiness, we will not fear making choices that keep us undefiled. We will run to the Lord for his help, cleansing, and strengthening in holiness. And the love he will pour out when we do so will only make us desire holiness more.

As a child I once had the misfortune of playing follow-the-leader with the neighborhood prankster. At that time in the South, new subdivisions were springing up like daisies, and storm drainage was a constant problem. Some developers simply ran open culverts into nearby woods to divert the run-off until a permanent solution could be found. My friend and I were playing near one of these open culverts—but I did not know it. My friend did.

It was late fall and in the woods leaves covered the ground and also the culvert. My "friend" (I use the word loosely), who happened to be the leader in the game at the time, led me toward the leaf-covered culvert. Running at full throttle, he sprang over the culvert and I, being unaware of its existence, ran just as fast but fell hard into that sewage-filled ditch. I was dirty, smelly, and humiliated. More than that, I was afraid of what my mother would do when she saw my filth.

I can remember walking down the street, my arms outstretched, dripping mud and slop in every step. I was so wet, so cold, so soiled—and crying all the way. With each step I got more scared and humiliated. My mom saw me coming. Seeing my tears and sensing my distress, she came out of the house. She ran to me and, instead of scolding me, knelt down and hugged me close. I had been in a sewer, and all she did was stoop down and hold me. She made herself filthy to comfort me.

As I felt that love wash me, I suddenly hated getting my mom dirty. I wanted so much not to have to make her bear any more. I told her she didn't have to touch me, but she hushed my protests and held me more. Then, even as I took comfort from her embrace, I wanted to spare her ever again from such defilement.

I recognize now that in my shame and in my mother's actions there was a reflection of the process of grace. Though the sewage of sin defiles each of us, Jesus kneels down from heaven to embrace us. He once dirtied himself by assuming the total shame of our sins on the cross. Even now he does not turn away from anyone, but holds close those who come to him though soiled and dirty. What must be our response to such sacrificial love? We must want to dirty him no more. If we see how great is the cleansing love of his embrace, our great desire is to bring no more filth upon him. We will want to spare him ever again from such defilement, not because he would otherwise love us less, but because in the light of the cross we love him more. We must so bask in his love that we want to bathe our relationship with him. The love of Christ constrains us to do his will as in gratitude we aspire to holiness. We resolve to remain undefiled for the sake of Jesus, who washes us with his blood and holds us in his love.

2

When the Bottom Falls Out

(Daniel 2)

The Word

Above all, the first chapter of Daniel displays God's honesty. Without sugar coating or fancy coloring, God plainly says that holiness carries risks. The second chapter of Daniel highlights the provision of the Lord. Here God is just as honest; the risks of holiness are just as plainly revealed. But now God not only prepares us to expect some trauma when holiness is pursued; he teaches us how to handle trauma when it comes. We are told that God will not leave us helpless. In this slice of Daniel's life, God gives us the weapons we need to stand for him when our holiness comes under assault.

> 1In the second year of his reign, Nebuchadnezzar had
> dreams; his mind was troubled and he could not sleep. 2So
> the king summoned the magicians, enchanters, sorcerers
> and astrologers to tell him what he had dreamed. When they
> came in and stood before the king, 3he said to them, "I have
> had a dream that troubles me and I want to know what it
> means."
>
> 4Then the astrologers answered the king in Aramaic, "O king, live forever! Tell your servants the dream, and we will interpret it."
>
> 5The king replied to the astrologers, "This is what I have firmly decided: If you do not tell me what my dream was and interpret it, I will have you cut into pieces and your houses

turned into piles of rubble. [6]But if you tell me the dream and explain it, you will receive from me gifts and rewards and great honor. So tell me the dream and interpret it for me."

[7]Once more they replied, "Let the king tell his servants the dream, and we will interpret it."

[8]Then the king answered, "I am certain that you are trying to gain time, because you realize that this is what I have firmly decided: [9]If you do not tell me the dream, there is just one penalty for you. You have conspired to tell me misleading and wicked things, hoping the situation will change. So then, tell me the dream, and I will know that you can interpret it for me."

[10]The astrologers answered the king, "There is not a man on earth who can do what the king asks! No king, however great and mighty, has ever asked such a thing of any magician or enchanter or astrologer. [11]What the king asks is too difficult. No one can reveal it to the king except the gods, and they do not live among men."

[12]This made the king so angry and furious that he ordered the execution of all the wise men of Babylon. [13]So the decree was issued to put the wise men to death, and men were sent to look for Daniel and his friends to put them to death.

[14]When Arioch, the commander of the king's guard, had gone out to put to death the wise men of Babylon, Daniel spoke to him with wisdom and tact. [15]He asked the king's officer, "Why did the king issue such a harsh decree?" Arioch then explained the matter to Daniel. [16]At this, Daniel went in to the king and asked for time, so that he might interpret the dream for him.

[17]***Then Daniel returned to his house and explained the matter to his friends Hananiah, Mishael and Azariah.*** [18]***He urged them to plead for mercy from the God of heaven concerning this mystery, so that he and his friends might not be executed with the rest of the wise men of Babylon.*** [19]***During the night the mystery was revealed to Daniel in a vision. Then Daniel praised the God of heaven*** [20]and said:

"Praise be to the name of God for ever and ever;
  wisdom and power are his.

21 He changes times and seasons;
he sets up kings and deposes them.
He gives wisdom to the wise
and knowledge to the discerning.
22 He reveals deep and hidden things;
he knows what lies in darkness,
and light dwells with him.
23 I thank and praise you, O God of my fathers:
You have given me wisdom and power,
you have made known to me what we asked of you,
you have made known to us the dream of the king."

24 Then Daniel went to Arioch, whom the king had appointed to execute the wise men of Babylon, and said to him, "Do not execute the wise men of Babylon. Take me to the king, and I will interpret his dream for him."

25 Arioch took Daniel to the king at once and said, "I have found a man among the exiles from Judah who can tell the king what his dream means."

26 The king asked Daniel (also called Belteshazzar), "Are you able to tell me what I saw in my dream and interpret it?"

27 Daniel replied, "No wise man, enchanter, magician or diviner can explain to the king the mystery he has asked about,
28 but there is a God in heaven who reveals mysteries. He has shown King Nebuchadnezzar what will happen in days to come. Your dream and the visions that passed through your mind as you lay on your bed are these:

29 "As you were lying there, O king, your mind turned to things to come, and the revealer of mysteries showed you what was going to happen.
30 As for me, this mystery has been revealed to me, not because I have greater wisdom than other living men, but so that you, O king, may know the interpretation and that you may understand what went through your mind.

31 "You looked, O king, and there before you stood a large statue—an enormous, dazzling statue, awesome in appearance.
32 The head of the statue was made of pure gold, its chest and arms of silver, its belly and thighs of bronze,
33 its legs of iron, its feet partly of iron and partly of baked clay.
34 While

you were watching, a rock was cut out, but not by human hands. It struck the statue on its feet of iron and clay and smashed them. [35]Then the iron, the clay, the bronze, the silver and the gold were broken to pieces at the same time and became like chaff on a threshing floor in the summer. The wind swept them away without leaving a trace. But the rock that struck the statue became a huge mountain and filled the whole earth.

[36]"This was the dream, and now we will interpret it to the king. [37]You, O king, are the king of kings. The God of heaven has given you dominion and power and might and glory; [38]in your hands he has placed mankind and the beasts of the field and the birds of the air. Wherever they live, he has made you ruler over them all. You are that head of gold.

[39]"After you, another kingdom will rise, inferior to yours. Next, a third kingdom, one of bronze, will rule over the whole earth. [40]Finally, there will be a fourth kingdom, strong as iron—for iron breaks and smashes everything—and as iron breaks things to pieces, so it will crush and break all the others. [41]Just as you saw that the feet and toes were partly of baked clay and partly of iron, so this will be a divided kingdom; yet it will have some of the strength of iron in it, even as you saw iron mixed with clay. [42]As the toes were partly iron and partly clay, so this kingdom will be partly strong and partly brittle. [43]And just as you saw the iron mixed with baked clay, so the people will be a mixture and will not remain united, any more than iron mixes with clay.

[44]"In the time of those kings, the God of heaven will set up a kingdom that will never be destroyed, nor will it be left to another people. It will crush all those kingdoms and bring them to an end, but it will itself endure forever. [45]This is the meaning of the vision of the rock cut out of a mountain, but not by human hands—a rock that broke the iron, the bronze, the clay, the silver and the gold to pieces.

"This great God has shown the king what will take place in the future. The dream is true and the interpretation is trustworthy."

[46]Then King Nebuchadnezzar fell prostrate before Daniel and paid him honor and ordered that an offering and incense

be presented to him. 47***The king said to Daniel, "Surely your God is the God of gods and the Lord of kings and a revealer of mysteries, for you were able to reveal this mystery."***

48Then the king placed Daniel in a high position and lavished many gifts on him. He made him ruler over the entire province of Babylon and placed him in charge of all its wise men. 49Moreover, at Daniel's request the king appointed Shadrach, Meshach and Abednego administrators over the province of Babylon, while Daniel himself remained at the royal court.

Daniel 2 (*Emphasis added*)

Strawberry Suds

A few weeks ago my wife came home from the weekly grocery trip with more than groceries to be concerned about. Kathy came into the house holding the lip of a full sack in one hand, balancing a crying baby on the other arm, and urging forward two frazzled preschool sons who were straggling behind. Just as she squeezed through the back door and inched around the dishwasher, the side of the discount-store paper sack ripped. Everything inside crashed to the floor, including a large, economy-size bottle of liquid dish soap. When the bottle hit the linoleum, the lid sprang off, and its innards gushed across the kitchen floor.

You know the responses that follow such a calamity. You put the crying baby (still crying) into her high chair. You tell the boys to jump over the puddle. And you run for the paper towels. Kathy did all that. But then, as she got down on her knees and started to sop up the soap, she noticed there was a strange hissing sound coming from the nearly forgotten grocery bag. The bag was still sitting half upright on the floor where it had crashed. Kathy looked inside what was left of the sack to see what was hissing. She found it. A two-liter, strawberry-soda bottle had ruptured inside the bag, which was now rapidly filling with the fizzy red liquid. Kathy grabbed the bottle and the few other items remaining in the sack and threw them into the sink. Then slowly, ever so carefully, she lifted the paper sack with its two-inch pool of soda at the bottom and headed for the sink. She never made it. Before she even took her first step, the bottom fell out. Carbonated strawberry juice and liquid detergent swirled around her feet. The result? Strawberry suds! The kids loved it. But not Mom!

What do you do when the bottom falls out? If the problem is a ruptured grocery sack, the remedy is plain enough. You get out the mop. But what do you do when the bottom falls out of your life—your career, your family's security, your health? What do you do when things just go haywire? You must not believe the unthinkable could not happen to you. The fact is, even believers face crises. Yes, the bottom can fall out for God's people. Christians may face crippling disappointment and disaster—every day may have "trouble of its own" (Matt. 6:34):

A teenage boy enters a hospital with breathing problems. The doctor suspects the problem is drug-related. The boy's Christian parents cannot believe it: they have never seen their son consume anything stronger than raspberry soda. But the doctor turns out to be correct.

A state school-board official, a lay leader in his church, is arrested for shoplifting a bottle of rosé wine. The police report says he took the bottle into the store's restroom, where he finished it off. How could this happen? He tells later of job pressures, personal medical problems, family discord, and, finally, a daughter's recently diagnosed brain tumor.

A seven-year-old girl is diagnosed as having leukemia. Her father, a believer, has just been laid off from his job.

A wonderful church elder, one of our dearest friends, watched sadly for over a year and a half as his only daughter's marriage disintegrated. Next he lost his job. And then his daughter was killed in a car wreck.

All these are real events. All involve real Christians. All remind us that the events of the second chapter of Daniel have a lot to do with today's realities. That's because the bottom fell out for Daniel, just as it did for the people above.

Daniel's Crisis

Not everything had been rosy in Daniel's life so far—the first chapter of his life history makes that clear. Although he had been born of royal Israelite lineage, a cruel and idolatrous despot had overrun Daniel's homeland and taken him captive. Still, events had been on the upswing of late. Because of his background and gifts Daniel won an appointment to train for the king's service. At the end of that training he had become superior to all his peers and even ten times wiser than the wise men of Babylon. So Daniel "entered the king's service," (1:19). We do not know all the responsibilities involved but that terminology is the same as is used to describe Joseph's duties when he became a governor for Pharaoh (Gen. 41:46). With God's help the young Jewish captive had risen above his circumstances. The future appeared secure. Then the bottom fell out.

The king had a dream. The dream troubled the king—in fact, it scared him. So he called in his wise men to find out what the dream meant.

"Tell us the dream, O king, and we will interpret it for you," the experts said.

"Oh, no," the king replied. "If you're so wise and all-knowing as you claim, *you* tell me what my dream is. Then, after you tell me what it means, I'll know if you really have any insight."

Of course, the counselors could not tell the king what his dream was. Their failure and their excuses so angered the king that he ordered all the wise men of the kingdom killed. But don't forget that Daniel was a wise man, too. In fact, he was the wisest. So the commander of the king's guard came looking for Daniel. In one hand this officer held a sword, in the other an order for Daniel's execution. By worldly measure, the bottom had fallen out for Daniel. It was all over. After much suffering, Daniel had regained some semblance of a decent life and all was about to end with one sword stroke.

What can we do when the bottom falls out? We want to cry, or yell in anger, or simply collapse. But Daniel's responses to crisis help us know the best things we believers can do when the bottom falls out of our world.

The Response of Prayer

Daniel's first spiritual response to his crisis appears in Daniel 2:17–18: "Then Daniel returned to his house and explained the matter to his friends Hananiah, Mishael and Azariah. He urged them to plead for mercy from the God of heaven concerning this mystery, so that he and his friends might not be executed with the rest of the wise men of Babylon."

When the bottom fell out, Daniel fell to his knees. He responded to crisis with prayer. Although he secured extra time from the king, that reprieve was not to cook up an escape plan. Daniel immediately gathered those who loved the Lord and urged fervent prayer.

Perhaps it does not strike you as significant that Daniel's first response to crisis was prayer. We tend to think of Daniel as a faith giant, one of those Old Testament saints who is *supposed* to pray, and frequently. Remember, though, if anybody had a reason to skip prayer—or pursue any number of other first responses—it was Daniel. He had other options. For one thing, he was sharp, ten times wiser than the wisest in Babylon. So he could have used his extra time to try to figure out some solution to his predicament. Besides his intelligence, Daniel had power. After all, he was in the king's service. Surely Daniel had learned to manage the politics of the royal court (the passage says he spoke to the commander of the guards with "wisdom and tact"). Maybe he could finagle something—call in some favors, pull a few strings, twist an arm. Daniel had the same choices of action we do. Yet in a crisis he chose prayer first.

Daniel's choice of prayer may seem obvious, but too often we do not follow Daniel's example in our crises, no matter how spiritually mature we may think we are. When I was pursuing graduate studies at a secular institution, I discovered how unpopular and dangerous Christian commitments can be. In my research work, I used an analytical method that reveals much about the way our minds assimilate information. Earlier researchers using this methodology assumed that there are no absolute truths—no real right or wrong—that everything is relative and subjective. As a Christian I had to reject those presuppositions. If the Bible is true, there *are* absolutes. When my "philosophical position" became known, I was told that a certain professor on my examining committee would likely block the awarding of my degree. Three years of work, hardship for my family, hundreds of pages of manuscript, thousands of hours of research, long-term career plans—all were about to go up in smoke. This was truly the bottom falling out.

So I got busy. I called my faculty adviser and made an appointment with the department chairman. I began taking steps to re-organize my examining committee. I even alerted my future employer that my credentials were in jeopardy. What was missing in all this frantic activity? Prayer, of course. It's not that I did not plan to pray. Oh, Bryan Chapell was going to get around to prayer, but prayer just didn't make it to the top of his "to do" list. Bryan Chapell had to handle this crisis on his own. Bryan Chapell had to grab the reins. Bryan Chapell was going to locate and organize the experts, the allies, the pathways, and all the means to fix *his* problem.

Not until I had stumbled for several days down *my* path of personal solution to the crisis did it hit me that I had not really prayed. Yes, I had whispered a few silent "help me's." But I had not fallen to my knees in concentrated, humble, dependent prayer. I had not gathered those who love the

Lord and love me to pray as Daniel did with his friends (2:18). I realize now that it is often not until we are serious about prayer that we involve others in our praying. Thankfully, despite my failings, the Lord did persuade Kathy and me of our need to pray—and finally we prayed—*together.*

The problem did not immediately go away. Until the day I orally defended my research before the examining committee, we knew there was a good chance I would be denied a degree because of my conviction that there *is* such a thing as absolute truth. Still, as aware as I was of the potential problems my Bible-based beliefs could cause, I was surprised that the very first question I was asked attacked my position head on.

As the opening question of my exam, the highest-ranking faculty member in the department asked, "How can you use this methodology, which assumes the relevance of truth, and at the same time have a commitment to particular truths?"

I gulped. So much for a nice, easy start. "Here we go down the tubes," I thought. Still, I answered as best I could. I explained that the methodology revealed much about how our minds function. I was not undermining the value of the research technique nor the results derived from it. I simply did not agree that one had to presuppose the relevance of truth to use this research tool.

Then a completely unexpected thing happened. The examiner, that most important committee member, simply said, "Okay." I could hardly believe my ears. The other committee members could hardly believe theirs. The ranking professor had simply said, "Okay"! Now any other professor who kept pressing me on the subject would be slapping the face of the most important examiner. After all, if the highest-ranking scholar had declared my argument satisfactory, no one could attack the argument without seeming to challenge the authority and competence of a senior faculty member. No one asked any more questions on that subject!

In the first five minutes of an exam that generally takes hours, we were done with the only question that could have jeopardized my degree. *I* could not have possibly arranged such a sequence of events. No matter what type of planning and politicking I attempted, I could not have arranged for that professor to ask that question at that moment, thereby blocking all further challenges. No, *I* could not. But God could—and God did. His abilities are beyond our imagining. His ways are beyond our knowing. His solutions are beyond our doing. That is why, when the bottom falls out, he urges us to seek him first.

We often forget how truly helpless we are apart from God. Our society constantly tells us that our own efforts are what make things happen. In the business world, in our families, even in the church, our activities and programs and planning are seen as the cause of success or of failure. So, when the bottom falls out of our lives, we instinctively turn to ourselves. We are so accustomed to depending on our own resources that we neglect seeking God's supply when we need it the most. This is even true of the clergy and other "professional" Christians.

Jack Miller, one of this nation's great pastors, once included a simple request in a letter to a friend of mine. The request revealed not only the sensitivity of this pastor's heart to God's Word, but also the poignant truth of our constant struggle to include God in our lives. Jack wrote, "Please pray for my habitual tendency to trust in myself and what I can do." Great men of God recognize the temptation to depend on themselves. We should all acknowledge that weakness in ourselves. We should take care not to become so busy, so accustomed to figuring our way out of crisis, that we forget God's way out: prayer.

Recently, a young man sat in my office. He was broke, out of work, and trying to find some direction for his life. According to society's agenda, he should have been traumatized and troubled, but he was bubbling with joy as he told his story:

> Pastor, for two months I've been doing everything possible I know to do to get back on track. I have tried to get a job,

using every skill I have. I have searched the want ads, hit the bricks, called all my contacts, mailed résumés, driven what seemed like a million miles. Nothing was happening. I was so wound up in job hunting that I didn't realize how spiritually dry I had become.

Then I realized I had not had a conversation with a Christian friend in weeks. My devotional life was "zilch." My church attendance was "in and out" as fast as I could manage, so I didn't waste any job-hunting time. I need God now more than I have ever needed him, but I wasn't even giving him a moment. When I realized that, it was as though I heard God say to me, "Stop trying to do this your way. Depend on me. Read my Word and talk to me."

Ever since that moment, I've been praying regularly, and it's hard to fathom the difference it's made. Suddenly God is opening doors I never dreamed would be opened for me. But, even more important than that, I realize now that God will provide for my needs even if all these doors close. For the first time in my life I know how good it feels to be absolutely confident in God.

Prayer represents the confession of our need for God. It does not mean that we are to become irresponsible about our duties, actions, and plans. But prayer does acknowledge our dependency: "Apart from you, Lord, my actions and plans mean nothing. On my own, Lord, I can't fix this. I can't put it together again, heal the wound, correct the fault, or clean up the mess. God, you must take control if any good is to result. Use me if you will, but you must do what I confess I cannot do alone, despite my power, my brains, and my connections. Only you, Lord, are truly able. I depend on you alone." When our hearts are committed to such truths, our actions will change. We will recognize that before we pick up the telephone, call the meeting, create the priority list, or form a crisis-management plan, we must fall to our knees and seek our God. He is the only effective crisis manager. As we confess our weakness to God, his ability and power are acknowledged and revealed.

You may fear to seek God in time of crisis if you have not sought him regularly before. But do not let that fear dissuade you from turning to him now and in the future. One of the beautiful messages in Daniel is that there is never a wrong time to pray. Daniel gathered his friends together for focused prayer *after* a crisis came. Daniel did not hesitate to approach God in more fervent prayer when circumstances were even more pressing. Any time is the right time to pray. Crisis can be the very instrument God is using to draw us to greater dependence on him. If the bottom has fallen out, and you have not prayed much before, pray now. When the bottom fell out in his life, prayer was Daniel's first response. If the bottom has fallen out for you, and prayer has not been your first response, make it your next one—and now!

The Response of Praise

This second chapter of this young prophet's life also describes a spiritual activity that should follow prayer during crisis. This activity should come as naturally as prayer, but it may be more difficult to imitate. The second desired response to crisis is recorded in Daniel 2:19–23:

> During the night the mystery was revealed to Daniel in a vision. Then Daniel praised the God of heaven and said:
>
> "Praise be to the name of God for ever and ever;
> wisdom and power are his.
> He changes times and seasons;
> he set up kings and deposes them.
> He gives wisdom to the wise
> and knowledge to the discerning.
> He reveals deep and hidden things;
> he knows what lies in darkness,
> and light dwells with him.
> I thank and praise you, O God of my fathers:
> You have given me wisdom and power,
> you have made known to me what we asked of you,
> you have made known to us the dream of the king."

In the midst of his crisis, Daniel offered personal praise to God; he opposed pressure with praise. "Oh, sure!" you may say. *After* God told Daniel what the king's dream was, when the crisis was over, only then did he praise God. It's easy to praise God if you get the answers." Still, before you turn away from Daniel's experience as an irrelevant story, think again about how God's answer affected him. Sure, he got the dream and its interpretation. But suddenly Daniel found himself facing a second crisis, which was potentially more threatening.

Nebuchadnezzar's dream entailed an enormous, dazzling statue. Its head was made of gold. The chest and arms were of silver; the belly and thighs were bronze; the legs were iron; the feet were iron and clay. In the dream a rock cut without human hands then struck the statue and pulverized it into dust, which the wind then swept away. Without any prompting, Daniel related this entire dream to the king. You can imagine the cruel king's response: "Hey, this Daniel is pretty good. He knows my dream even though I did not tell it to him." "Now," thinks the king, "I'll have him tell me what it means." Daniel *will* tell the king what the dream means—and there's the rub.

What did the dream mean? Bad news! The interpretation that Daniel had to give to this bloodthirsty king is recorded for us (2:39–45). Nebuchadnezzar's kingdom was to be divided. It was to be replaced by one kingdom after another until, eventually, all this king had amassed and built would be destroyed and scattered like chaff on the wind. Put yourself in Daniel's place. There is a death sentence already on your head. The commander of the king's guard, sword in hand, is at your side. Yet you are supposed to tell this ruthless king that he (and all he stands for) will soon amount to less than sweat on a flea.

Surely Daniel must have gulped a few times before offering this dire prediction to the king. Far from solving all Daniel's problems, God's revelation of the king's dream probably placed the prophet in even greater danger than the first crisis, when the king had ordered the deaths of all his wisemen. In the first crisis, Daniel was one among many wisemen in danger. He might have fled the city or slipped into a crowd unobserved. But now he stood alone before Nebuchadnezzar with a message almost guaranteed to anger and offend the tyrant. Daniel probably had never flirted so closely with death. So, ask yourself again: Was it really easy for Daniel to praise God once he had the dream's interpretation? Of course not.

There are three reasons Daniel could still praise God. First, although Daniel did not yet know how everything would work out, there was already *present* evidence of God's care. After all, God had revealed Nebuchadnezzar's dream. No other wiseman's god had come even close. God displayed his greatness and goodness to Daniel by simply letting his prophet see and understand the dream. What the interpretation of the dream would cause to happen in Daniel's life was still hidden, but grace was already evident in the crisis. Daniel knew what no one else had a clue about. There was enough present good to praise God even in the continuing press of crisis. Daniel did not ignore the crisis, but neither did he allow it to obscure the good. Daniel praised God for the good he could already see, despite the grace he could not yet fully anticipate or understand.

The second reason Daniel could praise God is that he could remember God's goodness in the *past.* The first chapter of Daniel's story revealed the faithfulness of God that had preserved Daniel and his friends to that point. No doubt it was God's past faithfulness to this loyal band that encouraged them to gather together in this new crisis and pray. God often points us to past grace to grant us reassurance and courage in present difficulties.

Daniel was not limited to past or present, however, in having cause to praise his God. The third reason for Daniel to praise the Lord stemmed from the interpretation of Nebuchadnezzar's dream: it unveiled a *future* good for which God deserved praise. The rock that "endures forever" after breaking in pieces the statue representing successive worldly kingdoms could be none other than our Rock, Jesus Christ. Through Nebuchadnezzar's dream, God showed Daniel the triumph of Christ and his kingdom.

To be candid, this revelation did not get rid of the present crisis. Daniel and his people were still in slavery. God's temple was still in ruins. God's prophet was still in jeopardy. Still, God displayed his long-range plans to Daniel. Although the young man did not know all that would happen in his immediate situation, God assured him that all things were working toward a grand triumph. So, despite his present danger, there was good in past, present, and future for which Daniel could praise God.

Likewise, God's goodness displays itself in our past, present, and future. Even in crises our lives are filled with countless reasons to praise God. Aspects of God's grace may remain hidden, but grace is still at work. One of the most vivid demonstrations of that fact came home to me when a young man (whom I'll call Richard) visited me.

Richard was a young husband, a new father, and a recent convert. He earned a big salary, and he and his wife lived lavishly, spending every penny they earned, plus more on credit. Now he had just learned that his employer was budget-tightening, and his job was about to be eliminated. The couple's house was mortgaged to the hilt. Their cars were both still being paid off. Without Richard's big paycheck, he and his family were about to lose everything.

There had been other recent losses in their lives as well. Through a series of discourtesies just prior to their conversion, the couple had alienated their closest relatives. Then the youth ministry the two had tried to start in their church had failed. Although they worked hard at it, they could not seem to establish a rapport with the high-schoolers or their parents. Whichever direction Richard looked as he examined his life, he saw only failure, rejection, and uncertainty. He talked to me for forty-five minutes, simply unloading his frustrations. Hurt, anger, and fear poured out of him. Richard wondered out loud why God seemed to be letting him down, now that he was just trying to turn his life around as a new believer.

After he finished unloading, Richard sank back into his chair, threw up his hands in frustration, and, speaking of his wife, said, "I just tell Betty that, regardless of what happens, at least we still have each other and kids we love." The sound of his despairing words silenced him. They were meant to accuse God, but instead they challenged Richard. In the quiet that followed his complaint, his mind began to replay those last words: "At least we still have each other and kids we love." Richard was remembering the years he and his wife had longed for children. Only a few months ago, it seemed, they had called it quits on their marriage and separated until the Lord used a pastor friend to draw them back to each other. The love this couple now shared was so beautiful and real that the past seemed almost like a nightmare from other people's lives. It was even hard for this young man to fathom again what his life had been like. But now, as he thought about his own words, he remembered it all.

Richard remembered the shambles in the silence his words had created. That silence made the final words echo all the more loudly: ". . . we still have each other and kids we love." Suddenly, the magnitude of that statement hit him. He bolted upright in his chair and with a sheepish grin said, "I guess God has been pretty good to us after all." When the bottom was falling out of his life, Richard praised God for the good he could see—despite the grace he could not yet see.

Having seen God's goodness to him in the past and present—and having praised God for it—something else happened to Richard. The very act of praising God produced in his heart courage to face the loss of his job. Praise arms God's people to face their foes. Praise so focuses our minds on the greatness of God that our trials are far less intimidating. Trials do not disappear because we praise God, but believers' hearts are healed from despair when they praise their God.

Richard ultimately was laid off for a time. His family did

struggle to maintain their home. They did lose one car. Their financial struggles did force them to cement some relationships with relatives. Most significant, however, this family learned it could live without some of the possessions they once considered essential. They re-evaluated their priorities and recommitted themselves to the Lord's purposes.

Eventually Richard was hired back, but he worked only a few months at his old job. He and his wife decided that if they could do without some material pleasures for a while, God might have a grander purpose for their lives. Today Richard is in seminary, studying for the ministry. There are still some financial trials, but this family is not despairing. They have seen the goodness of God. And they trust him for the grace they do not yet see. As they praise God for his past goodness, the praise itself grants assurance of grace for present and future trials. Praise is not a cure-all, of course. But, if you were to ask Richard what single incident had the greatest impact on his Christian life, he would tell you it was the moment he realized that the absence of income and possessions did not mean the absence of grace. The bottom never falls out of God's plan for a believer.

Perhaps the bottom has fallen out of your life. You do not know why. You cannot imagine any sensible explanation. It hurts. Maybe the problem is finances, or a family being torn apart, or a loved one or yourself so ill. How do you face the difficulty? Start by thinking of just one good thing God has put in your life right now. And then praise him for it. Next remember a second good thing God has done for you, but in the past. And praise him for that. Thank the Lord for the fact that he will yet do good things for you. Let the truths of Daniel's life assure you that when praise is in your heart, however deep is the darkness through which you walk, your hand is in God's. He has not departed. Praise him for the good you can see, knowing there is grace at work you may not yet see.

If there is no good you can identify in your life now (because life *can* seem that bleak), do not give up on the power of praise. The Bible is not asking us to look for "silver linings," it is allowing us to see God at work through the ages. What Daniel saw as future is, at least in part, already an element of your past. Daniel foresaw a rock made without human hands that would crush the powers of this world (2:44–45). This Rock of Salvation has already been revealed to us. Jesus came and conquered sin and death at Calvary, assuring us that he ultimately rules this world. Despite current hardships and heartaches, the greatest thing possible in all creation has occurred *already.* Jesus took others' sins on himself at Calvary and arose the Victor over them. As a believer, you are forgiven. As a child of the King, you need not live under guilt. God holds you in the hollow of his hand, and there is nothing that will occur in your life that God will not work for your ultimate good and his own glorious purpose (Rom. 8:28). This is adequate reason to praise God, even when present trials swirl around us.

But there is more! Through Nebuchadnezzar's dream, Daniel saw an *ultimate* and *eternal* victory of Christ over all the powers and dominions of this world. Christ's final work is not completed. Jesus is coming back to reign. All will be subject to his authority. Awaiting you is his kingdom, where there shall be no more tears or trials (Rom. 8:18; 2 Cor. 4:17; Rev. 21:4). Our trials will not last forever; his rule will be eternal. Unfairness, injustice, pain, and difficulty will end. All will be put right. For this future, too, we can praise God, even in present hardship. The present is bearable because ultimate and lasting glory is guaranteed.

The Response of Proclamation

Because he understood the nature of his Lord, Daniel offered prayer and praise to him in a difficult time. Still, Daniel's regard for God had yet to reach its broadest expression. When the bottom seemed to fall out, and Daniel's circumstances remained tough, *his third response to peril was proclaiming the greatness of God.* Daniel responded to peril with proclamation. The young prophet resisted any temptation to take credit for the amazing insight God granted him. Instead, he was careful to ensure that God alone was glorified (Dan. 2:27–28, 45c).

There is a set of stairs in our home that goes straight up between the first and second floors. There is no landing or turn to ease the steepness of the slope or shorten the number of steps down which a person might fall. Because our children are small, we sometimes worry about their safety on these stairs. Our daughter, who is still just a toddler, particularly concerns us. Simply because *we* worry, of course, does not mean the steps cause *her* the slightest concern. In fact, they seem to act like a magnet for her little body. She always wants to crawl up that stairway.

One day I caught her going up the stairs on her own. Normally she would get scolded for doing this, but this time she was trying so hard that I did not have the heart to stop her. I could not let her go alone, however, since there was too much danger. I quietly stepped behind her and held my hands inches from her diapered bottom in case she slipped. She was concentrating so much and grunting so loudly she did not notice me. Finally she reached the top of the stairs. You can hardly imagine how proud she looked as she walked around up there. If she could have talked, she would have crowed. It was as if every bone in her little body was saying, "Look what I did! I got up here all by myself." I guessed what she was thinking, but I had a rather different perspective. I knew that even if she thought she had made it alone, the truth was that other hands were at work, too. She was safe in the danger, not because of the grip of her infant hands on the steps, but because of the safety provided by the arms outstretched beneath her.

The Bible says that God is the One who keeps us safe, because beneath us are his "everlasting arms" (Deut. 33:27). We may think that what we have accomplished, or what we are as individuals is a matter of *our* efforts, arrangements, or abilities, but the truth lies in those other hands at work in our lives. Were it not for those hands beyond our own, we would long since have fallen from the heights we thought our abilities had enabled us to climb. Pride and self-acclaim disappear when the true source of human achievement is known. If we amount to anything, it is only because God climbed the heights with us and kept us from falling.

Daniel knew the truths of God's enabling and keeping. This knowledge erased all reference to self in his speech. The prophet was so conscious of his God's work that no explanation of the king's dream could omit the proclamation of God as the source of revelation. God could not be kept from Daniel's lips. As a result, God could not be kept from Nebuchadnezzar's mind. When Daniel finished interpreting the dream, Nebuchadnezzar not only rewarded Daniel but honored Daniel's God. The king said, "Surely your God is the God of gods, and the Lord of kings and a revealer of mysteries, for you were able to reveal this mystery" (v. 47). Because of Daniel's proclamation, the king knew that Daniel's ability was from his God. That Nebuchadnezzar recognized the power of God was an important product of Daniel's proclamation, one that would have far-reaching spiritual implications for this despot, as we shall see later.

But there were even more immediate implications. Daniel's proclamation, accompanying the revelation as it did, made the power and presence of the Lord so real that the king would not touch God's prophet. Daniel's interpretation openly downgraded the future of Babylon and her king. Yet, instead of ordering Daniel's execution for such an affront, Nebuchadnezzar fell prostrate before the prophet. The king was so humbled that the rage Daniel could rightly have expected never came. As Nebuchadnezzar bowed to Daniel, the proclamation itself became an instrument used by God to protect his prophet.

There is an important lesson for us all here. So often we neglect proclaiming God's omnipotence to those around us because we fear the testimony of our convictions will place us at some personal disadvantage. But Daniel's life makes clear that God chooses to work most powerfully when his name is most evident. We rob ourselves of God's power when we let circumstances steal his name from our lips. There is never a better time to proclaim God than when the risk seems great, because God assumes control of those causes fought in his name. The powers of this world cannot stand when God's glory is clearly, courageously, and openly declared.

Even when it does not make God's working become apparent to the world, the very act of proclamation strengthens believers in crisis. We know that Daniel had special insight into the nature and working of God. We should also recognize that Daniel's insights, and the strength he derived from them, always accompanied a passion to make God known to all. When we point others' eyes to the Lord, we see him more clearly ourselves.

We can bear almost anything if only we see God at work in our circumstances. Daniel teaches us that we may not see God clearly enough to take comfort and strength from that vision *until* we proclaim him to the world. Focusing others' eyes on God clarifies our vision of him. By expressing the nature of God to others, our own understanding of his will and ways grows. Hearts that overflow with the knowledge and love of God are never overwhelmed by the circumstances faith affirms are in his hands. Proclamation underscores the truths that strengthen our own hearts, minds, and spirits.

A Shift of Focus

Prayer, praise, and proclamation are all spiritual responses to crisis that shift attention from our abilities to God's. These responses humble us by making us realize we are ultimately dependent on God's power and influence rather than our own initiative. If we confess our human weakness in this way, God's strength will meet no barrier of pride in us. It is when we acknowledge a need greater than we can handle that God's supply is more sufficient than we can imagine.

There is always an element of our being that wants to take charge. When "the bottom falls out" in our lives, we recognize the futility of that attitude. Then we can discover that God is the only one who should be given charge of our lives and our difficulties. Not only can he alone handle all circumstances, he will work in them to lead us closer to himself. Extreme situations often reflect God's extreme desire for us to know his love more fully. He teaches us to lean on him, because—when we rest upon the One who loves us unconditionally—we know no greater peace nor can claim greater contentment. Such dependence upon God produces a joy so full that no crisis can exhaust its supply.

Knowing these truths, it is sometimes strange to discover how (despite our best intentions) we stop depending on God and resume trusting in human resources. Shortly after my wife and I left seminary, I became the pastor of an historic evangelical church in Illinois. The church was well established. My position was secure. We had a good income, lived in a nice house, and the friendly neighbors (who had a pool!) were even members of our church. Kathy and I said to one another, "We have struggled and pinched pennies long enough. Now, we have found the good life."

Partly because of our newfound security, we decided it was time to get our family started. This decision was not as easy for us as it may seem, because there is some history of birth disorders in my family. As Kathy was expecting our first child, we occasionally winced with inward pain when friends would say, "What do you want, boy or girl? Oh, it doesn't matter as long as the baby is healthy." Inside we thought, *What if our baby is* not *healthy*? We knew our child might have some problems. If that happened, were we supposed to feel sorry for ourselves? Would our child not be as precious as if he were perfect? Would our baby be worth less because of this universal prejudice for health? We resolved that our child would be priceless to us, regardless of what others might think.

As the time approached for the baby to be born, *we* began to prepare *ourselves* to love and value our child, who might be less than "perfect" by the world's standards. Finally, the due day arrived. Everything looked great. All the test results were good. The vital signs of mother and baby were normal. Then, just minutes before delivery, the monitors began to show that the baby was in distress.

When our son was born, he was blue—the result of oxygen deprivation. For some reason, in the last stages of delivery the baby did not get the oxygen he needed. The doctor tried to get him to breathe but with no success. We did not even get a chance to touch him before the nurses immediately took the baby to special equipment to clear his lungs and air passages. Because this was our firstborn, we did not fully understand what was happening. Then I saw one of the nurses look at the clock on the wall and begin timing our baby's *not* breathing. Now I knew what was happening. Inside, I cried, "Oh, heavenly Father, I thought I had prepared myself for anything, but I have not prepared for my child to die."

What thoughts go through your mind when your baby starts to die? You suddenly realize how helpless you are, that you cannot do anything to preserve what is dearest to you. You see that all your abilities, your preparations, your plans, really mean nothing. You are not in control. So what do you do? What *can* you do but pray! So I prayed, "God, help him. God, help us. I'm not sure what we will do, or what we will be, if we lose him. God, please save him."

God did save our child. Praise God!

I can praise God now for his past goodness to our family. There are still some hard times when I am tempted to think that God is not concerned for us—when grace seems far away and not very clear. But, in those times, I can look at the face of my beautiful, healthy child and praise my God.

Of course, I recognize that the health of my son is not, and cannot be, the only reason I praise God. Life is long and our young family has much yet to face. We face what is to come, however, with a greater understanding of our God, in part because of the perilous nature of our first son's birth.

But there is yet more to learn in the provision of a son. God spared *my* son, but he did not spare his own. I only began to anticipate the pain of the death of a son. God knows that pain. Although he was in control and not required to feel any pain, my God sacrificed his only Son for a sinner like me and like you. May God help us all never to lose sight of that great gift so that, when the bottom seems to fall out of our lives, we know what to do—whom to trust, whom to glorify, whom to affirm for others. When our focus is upon the cross rather than upon our crisis, our hearts will lead us to the One who purchased our lives with his own. We will *pray* to the God who loves us. We will *praise* the God who alone can save us. We will *proclaim* the God who gave his Son for us. Those three responses, which Daniel revealed for us a distant yesterday, will grant us peace for today and confidence for tomorrow: prayer, praise, and proclamation.

3

Faith in the Furnace

(Daniel 3)

The Word

Now the spotlight shifts. The focus moves from Daniel to his friends: Shadrach, Meshach, and Abednego. The emphasis changes from *actions* that result from faith to *attitudes* that characterize faith.

Despite his recent theology lesson from Daniel, Nebuchadnezzaar reverted to idolatry. The king erected an immense statue of gold and ordered all his subjects to bow down and worship the idol whenever the bands of the kingdom played a salute. Those who disobeyed would be thrown into a fiery furnace. At least three subjects did not heed the warning or bow to the idol. Shadrach, Meshach, and Abednego stood up for their God. By doing so, they got a blast of the king's wrath. In their response to Nebuchadnezzar, we see not only a model of human faithfulness, but learn what biblical faith truly is.

> 1King Nebuchadnezzar made an image of gold, ninety feet
> high and nine feet wide, and set it up on the plain of Dura
> in the province of Babylon. 2He then summoned the satraps,
> prefects, governors, advisers, treasurers, judges, magistrates
> and all the other provincial officials to come to the dedication
> of the image he had set up. 3So the satraps, prefects, gover-
> nors, advisers, treasurers, judges, magistrates and all the
> other provincial officials assembled for the dedication of the
> image that King Nebuchadnezzar had set up, and they stood
> before it.

[4]Then the herald loudly proclaimed, "This is what you are commanded to do, O peoples, nations and men of every language: [5]As soon as you hear the sound of the horn, flute, zither, lyre, harp, pipes and all kinds of music, you must fall down and worship the image of gold that King Nebuchadnezzar has set up. [6]Whoever does not fall down and worship will immediately be thrown into a blazing furnace."

[7]Therefore, as soon as they heard the sound of the horn, flute, zither, lyre, harp and all kinds of music, all the peoples, nations and men of every language fell down and worshiped the image of gold that King Nebuchadnezzar had set up.

[8]At this time some astrologers came forward and denounced the Jews. [9]They said to King Nebuchadnezzar, "O king, live forever! [10]You have issued a decree, O king, that everyone who hears the sound of the horn, flute, zither, lyre, harp, pipes and all kinds of music must fall down and worship the image of gold, [11]and that whoever does not fall down and worship will be thrown into a blazing furnace. [12]But there are some Jews whom you have set over the affairs of the province of Babylon—Shadrach, Meshach and Abednego—who pay no attention to you, O king. They neither serve your gods nor worship the image of gold you have set up."

[13]Furious with rage, Nebuchadnezzar summoned Shadrach, Meshach and Abednego. So these men were brought before the king, [14]and Nebuchadnezzar said to them, "Is it true, Shadrach, Meshach and Abednego, that you do not serve my gods or worship the image of gold I have set up? [15]Now when you hear the sound of the horn, flute, zither, lyre, harp, pipes and all kinds of music, if you are ready to fall down and worship the image I made, very good. But if you do not worship it, you will be thrown immediately into a blazing furnace. Then what god will be able to rescue you from my hand?"

[16]Shadrach, Meshach and Abednego replied to the king, "O Nebuchadnezzar, we do not need to defend ourselves before you in this matter. [17]If we are thrown into the blazing furnace, the God we serve is able to save us from it, and he will rescue us from your hand, O king. [18]But even if he does not, we want you to know, O king, that we will not serve your gods or worship the image of gold you have set up."

[19]Then Nebuchadnezzar was furious with Shadrach, Meshach and Abednego, and his attitude toward them changed. He ordered the furnace heated seven times hotter than usual
[20]and commanded some of the strongest soldiers in his army to tie up Shadrach, Meshach and Abednego and throw them into the blazing furnace.
[21]So these men, wearing their robes, trousers, turbans and other clothes, were bound and thrown into the blazing furnace.
[22]The king's command was so urgent and the furnace so hot that the flames of the fire killed the soldiers who took up Shadrach, Meshach and Abednego,
[23]and these three men, firmly tied, fell into the blazing furnace.

[24]Then King Nebuchadnezzar leaped to his feet in amazement and asked his advisers, "Weren't there three men that we tied up and threw into the fire?"

They replied, "Certainly, O king."

[25]He said, "Look! I see four men walking around in the fire, unbound and unharmed, and the fourth looks like a son of the gods."

[26]Nebuchadnezzar then approached the opening of the blazing furnace and shouted, "Shadrach, Meshach and Abednego, servants of the Most High God, come out! Come here!"

So Shadrach, Meshach and Abednego came out of the fire,
[27]and the satraps, prefects, governors and royal advisers crowded around them. They saw that the fire had not harmed their bodies, nor was a hair of their heads singed; their robes were not scorched, and there was no smell of fire on them.

[28]Then Nebuchadnezzar said, "Praise be to the God of Shadrach, Meshach and Abednego, who has sent his angel and rescued his servants! They trusted in him and defied the king's command and were willing to give up their lives rather than serve or worship any god except their own God.
[29]Therefore I decree that the people of any nation or language who say anything against the God of Shadrach, Meshach and Abednego be cut into pieces and their houses be turned into piles of rubble, for no other god can save in this way."

[30]Then the king promoted Shadrach, Meshach and Abednego in the province of Babylon.

Daniel 3 (*Emphasis added*)

A New Definition of Faith

How do you win the World Series? As I type these words, my favorite baseball team is near winning the National League pennant. If I could figure out how this team could become world champions, I would be the hometown hero and rich as well. Unfortunately for me, more credible characters have already publicized their "secret of success." A few years ago, when the New York Mets were the underdog darlings of the National League, two young pitchers told us how they were going to win the World Series. The pitchers were Tom Seaver and Tug McGraw. Borrowing a line from a Walt Disney character, they said the secret to winning the World Series is in these words: "Ya gotta believe."

Some clever advertising agency picked up that phrase, too, but in another context. According to one TV commercial, you make peanut butter "with a whole lot of peanuts and a little bit of magic" and, then, one more thing—"Ya gotta believe."

There appears to be a consensus in our culture that good things happen just because someone believes long enough and hard enough. Someone has enough faith that something will happen, so it does! Unfortunately, that notion about why good things happen is often transferred without serious thought to spiritual matters, which are also framed in terms of faith and belief. Christians sometimes assume that good things happen because of an exceptional confidence in an outcome they desire. We may even have been taught at some time in our Christian lives that if we want something to happen, it will come about when we build up enough faith. It is as if putting enough faith nickels in the celestial vending machine on high gets you what you want. At times the message sounds inviting and may even seem to work. But is it true? Is it biblical?

Many Christians do believe the Bible teaches that faith is merely the equivalent of confidence in outcomes. When talking about the miracles of the Bible, we can often point to those holy men and women of ancient times and say, "What great faith they had. Look at the wonderful things that happened because of their unwavering confidence in what would occur." But if this is your entire view of what biblical faith is, the third chapter of Daniel will disturb you.

This chapter of Daniel's history tells us of three faith giants: Shadrach, Meshach, and Abednego. These three young men are heroes of courage, obedience, and faith. They stood up to the cruel and wicked Nebuchadnezzar, refusing to bow to his image of gold, even when their lives were at stake. Yet, when Shadrach, Meshach, and Abednego stood on the brink of being thrown into the fiery furnace because of their faith commitment, they did not pretend to know what was going to happen to them. Although the three had no desire to burn, they did not claim they would not die. Instead of offering some confident assertion about what would occur because of their great faith, these men simply said in effect: "We really don't know what will happen; we only know we will obey God and trust him" (see Dan. 3:16–18).

Shadrach, Meshach, and Abednego did claim that God was *able* to save them and would, in fact, rescue them from the king's hand (because even if they died, they were still in God's hands). But, the three faithful men also said, even *if* God did *not* save them from the furnace of fire, they would worship only him (v. 18). These words may trouble you. Perhaps you want to say, "Oh, no, Shadrach, Meshach, and Abednego! No ifs, ands, or buts. Believe without doubting." But those three men did not operate on some popular notion of what faith should be. Theirs was a *biblical* faith.

By their words and actions, Shadrach, Meshach and Abednego tell us what biblical faith is and also what it is not. Biblical faith is not a belief that *we* know what is best; it is the belief that only *God* knows what is best. This is true faith, the confidence that God will always do what is right. We will serve him because we trust him—whatever happens. This new definition of faith is not gleaned from a popular consensus but from biblical evidence. The Bible says that faith is not confidence in a desired outcome to a particular circumstance. Instead, faith is confidence in God.

What good is such a definition of faith? Can it help us as we face today's trials? To answer, let me re-create a rainstorm experience from my college days. The storm may seem light-years from Nebuchadnezzar's human incinerator, but both taught me much about the difference between popular belief and biblical faith.

I had found a summer job working as an assistant to a commercial photographer who had been hired by a local pool manufacturer to create an advertisement with lots of photographs. We needed two full days of good weather to take all the shots necessary, and my boss, a Christian, encouraged me to pray with him for clear skies. So we prayed, and the first day of picture shooting was sunny, dry, and beautiful. One more day of such weather and we would be set.

It was not meant to be. The next day was dark, wet, and ugly. Sitting in my boss's station wagon that morning, I saw his face change slowly from sadness, to dejection, and then to anger. "Yesterday," he snarled, "God gave us a good day because we prayed in faith. Today it's raining even though we need it to be sunny. That means somebody isn't doing his job."

Now I don't know which "somebody" he had in mind and wasn't about to ask, but there were only two alternatives. Assuming that the first good day was because of our so-called faith, the reason the second day was rainy was either that our faith had shrunk or God had failed. Either we weren't doing our job, or God wasn't doing his.

Notice that to accept either alternative as truth is a mistake that can result in great harm. If our God is inadequate, we have no one to trust. If inadequate faith is what causes bad things to happen, no one really has sufficient faith, because everyone faces problems. If we link the degree or quality of faith to easy times and happy endings, we set ourselves up for doubt and heartache, because difficulty invades every life, including the faithful. Sometimes we can be so hard on ourselves and others, simply because we let other people tell us what "faith" is, rather than listening carefully to the Bible.

What Biblical Faith Is Not

One way to get a better picture of biblical faith, the kind that helps rather than harms—the kind that Shadrach, Meshach and Abednego shared—is to gain a clear understanding of what biblical faith is *not*.

Faith Is Not *Trust in Our Belief*

So often in Christian circles we link the effectiveness of our faith and our prayers to how strongly we can convince ourselves that there will be a positive outcome to a particular situation. We decide to let no doubt enter our minds. Some of us go through intricate rituals to convince ourselves that we have pumped up our faith enough for God to honor our desires. We sing songs, pray frequently, read more Scripture, scold ourselves for any wavering second thoughts, and try to convince ourselves that we believe as much as is necessary to get God to do what we think is right. In one sense we are like athletes psyching up for the big event—convincing ourselves that we really and truly believe. In another sense we resemble witches, throwing a pinch of song, an ounce of prayer, and a ton of belief into a caldron of human desires so that God *must* do what we determine is right for him to do. But that kind of faith is not so much trust in God's wisdom and power as it is confidence in the amount of belief we have conjured in an attempt to control him.

I recently heard a dear Christian mother express what can happen to our faith if we ever begin to trust in the degree of our belief rather than in God. This young mother was running errands one weekday morning with a tribe of preschoolers in the car. After the first few stops, she recognized she was running terribly late. She would miss a doctor's appointment if she couldn't make faster progress. Then came inspiration—a way to get back on schedule. The next stop on the errand list was the grocery store. Getting all of the young children out of their car seats, into their jackets, into the store, and then reversing it all when coming out, was bound to turn this into a twenty-minute stop, even though only a few groceries were needed. But, she thought, if there was a parking space right by the entrance, so she could watch the children through the storefront glass, she could leave the kids in the car. Mom could zip in, zip out, and be right back on schedule.

"Lord, thank you in advance," the young woman had prayed. "I believe you will give me a parking space. I believe." Recounting the experience later, she said, "I was praying with all kinds of faith and I *did* believe God would help me out!"

Her faith was dependent on convincing herself that she had enough belief to convince God to do what she wanted him to do. She drove to the store, turned in the parking lot, and saw immediately that there was no parking space anywhere near the entrance. You may smile at this young mother's naiveté. But, when she told of this small event in her life, she spoke through tears: "What's wrong with me? I prayed with everything I had, and God didn't answer. Don't I have enough faith?"

This Christian had caught herself in that old trap of trusting in belief, rather than trusting in God. Because her faith was dependent on seeing a positive outcome to her immediate circumstances, when something unwanted occurred she could only assume there was something lacking in her faith or something wrong with her God. Since she was too well schooled to believe that God could fail at anything, she assumed that she was at fault. Simply because what she wanted to happen did not, she thought her faith was inadequate or gone completely. But she had not lost her faith; she had misplaced it.

What precipitated the spiritual crisis in this young woman's life was the idea that faith resides in feelings of belief that we conjure in our minds. But faith is not a mind game. It is not an intellectual conclusion, a confident anticipation about things we would like to happen. Shadrach, Meshach, and Abednego said, "We don't know what will happen." Yet they were great men of faith. They understood that faith is not confidence in the appropriateness of our desires or the degree of our feelings. Real faith locks on to God, knowing that God will do what is appropriate and right regardless of our wishes. Shadrach, Meshach, and Abednego said that even if God would not deliver them, they wanted to serve only him. Their words tell about a faith measured not by the strength of human expectations, but by an abiding conviction that whatever God ordains is right.

Biblical faith calls for each of us to acknowledge God's provision as sufficient, loving, and good, even if it falls short of (or contradicts) our immediate desires, which can neither fully anticipate his plans nor fathom his wisdom. Believers whose faith can withstand the trials of this world affirm that, "I may not understand God's provision. I may not expect it or know enough in this life even to like it, but I trust my God in whatever comes. I will not always know what will come, but my faith is in my God, since he knows what is best.

This insight into faith relieves those who worry that there is something wrong with them or their faith quotient because what they want to happen does not always occur. The fact is, we are not inferior Christians when we trust God's wisdom more than our own. That's as it should be!

For too long, too many have been victims of the hoax that *real* Christians have no problems. If we are truly faithful believers, some imply, bad things will not happen to us. After all, sufficient faith solves all problems, doesn't it? Such a presentation of Christianity makes it seem sinful to weep, or hurt, or be disappointed. These emotions automatically imply that something has happened other than what we wanted and therefore supposedly demonstrate that our faith must be inferior. As a result of this flawed logic, we are inundated with literature and programming that extols the singular benefits and exclusive value of "enthusiastic Christianity." This brand of religion rides the waves of emotional highs, continuous smiles, and bubbling optimism. Of course, there is nothing wrong with any of these expressions—solemnity is no more holy than enthusiasm—unless it is implied that emotional highs measure one's faith level. Faith in Jesus Christ is not a feeling. Circumstances change feelings. Emotional tides surge and then recede with life's ups and downs. But just because feelings change does not necessarily mean faith wavers.

Shadrach, Meshach, and Abednego did not bubble with enthusiasm. Nowhere during this incident did any of the three say, "Oh, boy, here we go into the fiery furnace! Isn't this great?" They were not filled with enthusiasm about going into the furnace. They were not even confident about what would happen to them. But they *were* filled with faith in their God. They believed in his presence and in his care despite the likelihood that Nebuchadnezzar would burn them alive. If they lived, they would know their God was near. If they died, they would know their God was no more distant. Like Job, they would say of God, "Though he slay me, yet will I trust him."

God is loving, gracious, and good. Shadrach, Meshach, and Abednego knew that time after time God had delivered his people from their enemies despite Israel's sin and rebellion. There was no doubting the love of this God who had been faithful even when his people had not. God had even promised to save his people from this captivity in Babylon. Although things looked awfully grim in the immediate situation, the faith of these young men was unshattered, because it was not rooted in present circumstances but in the nature of their God and his loving and eternal purposes. Shadrach, Meshach and Abednego were not great men of faith because they were confident of easy living, or good times, or favorable circumstances, but rather because they trusted that God would accomplish his good purposes through them if they remained faithful.

This can be your great confidence, too. You can begin to see that tragedy does not mean God has vanished or deserted you (or that your belief is too weak). Danger does not indicate he has failed. Difficulty does not imply he is weak. God is always in control, and because you and I know his loving nature, we have faith that there is a plan and a purpose for whatever we face as individuals. Difficulties may still arise, but he will enable us to surmount or endure them. Grief may still come, but he will give us the strength to bear it. God's guiding hand is never capricious nor clumsy. True faith acknowledges that God knows all and is doing what is right. A faith that insists God must do things *our* way is flawed, since it is relying on human frailty and thus will lead only to disappointment and pain.

In a rural community where I once pastored a church, a family grew dissatisfied with the church across town, which they felt had lost its spiritual heading. So they set up a church in their home. Here the family taught that God would make folks rich and keep them healthy, *if* they had enough faith. They were not speaking without some "proof" to back up their words. For several years this farming family had been under contract with a large feed company to produce large quantities of hay and grain at a guaranteed price. Thus, while other farmers in the area suffered under the vagaries of a vacillating farm market, this family prospered. And any who visited their home to attend church were told the reason for their wealth: great faith.

Some of the family members so believed in the power of faith to gain earthly desires that they began to visit the sick in town. They would tell these ill persons, members of our church and others, that the reason they were ill was that they didn't have enough faith. After all, they reasoned, faith makes difficulty vanish. So if you are ill, you must be lacking in faith.

I do not doubt that this family from the new "church"

meant well. They were sincere in their intentions, but the consequences of their actions were horrible. For example, people who were terminally ill, who needed the Lord's comfort more than ever, were told they did not really know him at all. The evidence of that was their illness! Needless to say, on some of my pastoral calls after visits by these family members, I found Christian believers terrified and distraught because of this warped evaluation of their faith. My concern was not limited to the sick individuals the family visited, especially when the heartache came home to strike.

A child with a birth defect was born to one of the family members, and relatives claimed there must be sin in the lives of the parents of this child because otherwise the defect would go away. Those parents eventually left their family's church because there they found their faith constantly questioned on account of their child.

More problems followed for this misguided family when our community, like farm communities all over the country in the 1980s, sank into a financial crisis. Suddenly the production requirements of the big feed company became impossible for the wealthy family's farm to meet. The same contract that had provided security and prosperity for years now became a financial noose around the family's neck. In just a few months the business was bankrupt, the farm (which had been in the family for generations) was sold, and family members scattered to seek a living wage. Today they no longer visit hurting people and say, "Look at the health and wealth that comes from our faith."

We can take no joy in the pain this family experienced. Rather, we must grieve for them, even as we learn from them that faith in faith alone scatters families and shatters lives. Possessing real biblical faith—the kind that trusts God's power and purposes—is just as important today as it was in the day of Shadrach, Meshach, and Abednego. We live in a fallen world where illness, difficulty, and tragedy still thrive. Christians are not immune from the consequences of being in this world. God can remove disease and pain from our lives today if he chooses to do so—or he may desire to use our testimonies in the midst of trial and tragedy for purposes grander than we can see or even imagine. The decision is his. Our job is to trust him. Real faith is not trust in our belief, but confidence in God.

Faith Is Not *Trust in What We Want to Happen*

Although you may begin to see that faith is an expression of utmost confidence in God, it is possible still to believe that God should do what you think he should do. Even if you have avoided the misconception of thinking that true faith is a matter of how intensely you believe, you may run into another error that can damage your faith. Have you ever found yourself trusting God to do some very "spiritual" thing that *you* have decided he needs to do? We all sometimes begin counting on what we would love to happen, simply because we think it is in God's best interests to make it happen. Because the results we desire are "for God's sake," or for what we think will benefit another person, we are convinced they *must* occur.

Some years ago, my brother was in the Air Force and hurrying back to base to avoid being A.W.O.L. He faced a number of obstacles: he was traveling late at night, on a holiday weekend, in a pickup almost out of gas, during the Arab oil embargo when gas was hard to find. An unbelieving friend was riding with him. When this friend saw the gas needle land on empty, he threw up his hands in resignation and said, "That's it. We're never going to make it. We are in trouble, for sure."

My brother, concerned not only for getting back to base but for the spiritual welfare of his buddy, replied, "No, we are going to make it. I have prayed to God in faith. He will get us there."

You can guess what happened. A few miles further, the engine sputtered, coughed, and died. The story seems funny now, but at that time the humor was lost on my brother. This series of events was part of a serious spiritual crisis in his life.

"Bryan," he asked me later, "why didn't God answer my prayer? I prayed in faith, believing God. Nothing better could have happened for my friend than for him to see God at work. He would have believed in God and been saved if only God had answered my request. Why didn't God act?"

I do not know why God does not always grant our fervent requests. But I do know that biblical faith keeps us from being so attached to what we want (even if we are convinced that it is for God's good) that failing to get what we want constitutes a spiritual disaster. Faith is trust in God and his plan. Faith does not require God to fulfill wishes as though our desires were his command and our human plans his divine ordinance. God knows what is necessary to further his purposes and bring others to himself, including *when* it is necessary and *how* it should be done. Faith does not require God to do what we would love to happen, even when we think we have the right reasons.

Learning to trust God's wisdom above our own is not a lesson only those who are young in the faith must master. In times of trouble a willingness to rely solely on God's wisdom tries the faith of even the most spiritually astute. The Reverend Jim Conway is a wonderful pastor and author whom God has greatly used in a variety of ministries. A few years ago, when Jim was pastoring People's Bible Church in Urbana, Illinois, his daughter, Becki, was stricken with cancer. The doctors said they would have to amputate one leg to save her life. So the family began to pray, asking God to heal Becki's leg. They knew that God is able to heal, so they prayed that he would save her leg as a testimony of his love. Because they sincerely desired glory for God, they believed that God would heal Becki.

So strongly did Jim believe that God would honor the family's request that, on the day of the scheduled surgery, he asked the doctors to test Becki's leg again before amputating. The surgeon agreed, and the family went to a waiting room, eagerly anticipating the results they were sure would bring great glory to God and great joy to them. Jim later recounted for *Moody Monthly* what happened:

> A crowd of friends from the church had come to wait with us. So many came, in fact, that they made us leave the waiting room. When the surgeon came out, I knew what he was going to say, and I couldn't face it. I couldn't face all those people. So I ran.
>
> I ran to the hospital basement where no one would find me. And I cried. I yelled. I pounded my fists against the wall. I felt like the God whom I had served had abandoned me at the hour of my deepest need. Was he so busy answering prayers for parking places that he couldn't see Becki?

The experience devastated Jim, but it also drove him back to the Scriptures. There he discovered the problem implicit in a faith that blindly insists on what we would love to happen—even if what we want would seem to honor God. Such a faith is foreign to the Bible! You and I know that already, but in the pressure of the moment and under an aching desire for something that seems so right, we sometimes forget. We forget the faithful men and women of the Bible who did not have everything go as their desires dictated. We must remember them again, lest we define faith in such a way that we and others are hurt and disillusioned.

No one doubts the faith of the apostle Paul, probably the greatest missionary of all time and an inspired theologian. He opened the gospel to the Gentiles, wrote holy scriptural letters, and performed miraculous healings. Yet the Bible records at least four examples of sickness or disaster in Paul's life that God did not prevent. In 2 Corinthians 12:7–9, we are told that Paul prayed three times that God would remove a "thorn in my flesh," an affliction of some kind. We do not know precisely the ailment. What we do know is that God did not grant Paul's request but replied, "My grace is sufficient for you, for my power is made perfect in weakness."

Paul did not respond by doubting his faith or his God.

The apostle understood that his faith would not remove all hardship and suffering from his life. He believed that God knew what was best for him and for the ministry of the gospel. Thus, if God's strength was made more evident by having Paul give his testimony in a weakened condition, Paul readily accepted the disability and even rejoiced in his weakness, with the faith that God knows what is best. Paul's attitude reminds us that God knows far better than we what will bring men and women to a saving knowledge of himself. Sometimes the most powerful testimony Christians have is not the fact that they live on Easy Street, but that they are sustained by God when their worlds collapse—when they, like Paul, can say, "For when I am weak, then I am strong" (v. 10).

If genuine faith brings an end to all life's hardships, then Paul's comments in the chapter preceding the reference to the "thorn in my flesh" would also make no sense. In 2 Corinthians 11, Paul gives a virtual litany of his sufferings. He says he had been imprisoned, flogged, stoned, shipwrecked, sea-logged; endangered by bandits, countrymen, and threatening circumstances of all sorts; sleepless, hungry, thirsty, cold, naked and pressured by church concerns (vv. 23–28). How might we respond to such hardships in the life of an apostle? Should we say, "Now, Paul, if you just had a little more faith, life wouldn't be so hard." Of course not. We know the apostle's faith was sufficient for his hard times. More importantly, he did not *expect* his faith to keep him from hard times. Why, then, today do we sometimes believe that when times are hard in our lives or in the lives of "good people" we know, faith is in short supply?

Paul once encouraged Timothy to stop drinking only water and use a little wine because of the young pastor's stomach ailments (1 Tim. 5:23). I do not mention this to start a debate on the use of beverage alcohol, but to ask why Paul would give "medical advice" if he was truly an apostle. Why didn't Paul just heal Timothy? The solution seems so obvious, and certainly Paul had been used of God to heal on other occasions (e.g., Acts 14:8–10). Another time in his ministry Paul even raised a young man from the dead (Acts 20:7–12). Why not heal now? Should we assume that Paul was lacking in faith at this stage in his life? No, Paul's faith was alive and well. Remember, at the very moment Paul was writing this prescription, he was also writing inspired Scripture. Should we then assume that Timothy's faith was in question? No, Paul commended Timothy in this letter and gave him additional pastoral instruction. If Paul felt Timothy to be insufficiently faithful, surely the apostle would have rebuked the young man and suggested some spiritual strengthening. But there was no such correction. Why, then, did not Paul heal Timothy? We don't know. All we do know is that both Timothy and Paul continued to trust God's wisdom and purpose (2 Tim. 1:1–2, 5). To them illness was not an automatic sign of weakened faith.

Another example of the truth that being denied what we want does not mean faith is lacking lies in 2 Timothy 4:20. There Paul makes a passing reference to the fact that he left a disciple named Trophimus "sick in Miletus." Our minds do mental flips when we read these words, particularly if we believe that sincere faith rescues from all ills. "Why, Paul," we ask, "did you *leave* him sick? Why didn't you heal Trophimus?" There are no simple answers to such questions. Neither Paul nor Trophimus are said to have failed the Lord. Both have been identified, without qualification, as faithful followers of Jesus. We are left only with the understanding that here, as at other times in Paul's ministry, illness was a problem for Paul (Gal. 4:13–14) and for other believers, just as it is today. But it was not a problem that impugned faith. Rather, these difficulties required trust and produced even higher levels of faith, so that God's work might continue despite the trials people in all ages must confront.

The eleventh chapter of Hebrews is often called "the faith chapter" because it cites believers from many periods of biblical history who are famous for their faith. Added to the list of those well known for this quality are descriptions of unnamed faithful who have suffered great hardships. These anonymous men and women—who have been tortured, flogged, imprisoned, stoned, pierced with swords, sawed in two, or made destitute, deprived, and homeless—are all commended for their faith (Heb. 11:35–40). The New Testament writers never contend that the presence of difficulty in a life experience indicates an absence of faith in that individual.

Not even the greatest of Old Testament saints had a faith that removed every human trial. Remember Elisha, a faithful prophet of God? Like his predecessor, Elijah, he performed amazing miracles, routed armies, healed the sick, and raised the dead. But, unlike Elijah, he was not taken to heaven in a fiery chariot. Instead, without a word of criticism of his faith, the Scriptures simply record that Elisha got sick and died (2 Kings 13:14, 20). So faithful was Elisha to the Lord's work that even after he died his bones had healing powers (v. 21). The Bible never even implies that illness is necessarily a sign of faithlessness or that other difficulties prove either diminished spiritual integrity or a withdrawal of divine power and concern.

Finally, lest we begin to look for reasons to blame Paul, Elisha, or other biblical believers for their troubles, we should remember the example of Jesus himself. Did not Jesus pray before his crucifixion that God might take "this cup" from him? Still, the trial came. But, of course, there was no lack of faith on the Savior's part. His faith was focused on his Father's plans. He not only prayed that the cup be taken away "if it is possible," but added, "Yet not my will, but thy will be done." Although Christ wanted the trial to be taken away or to be unnecessary, his deepest desire was that God would work his perfect will, even if it meant humiliation and torture.

Christ's prayer teaches us what faith truly is. Faith is not to be a mental or emotional snapping of our fingers to get God to do what we think he should do. Our confidence should be in who God is. Edith Schaeffer says simply, "We must let God be God." We cannot presume to direct God's will as if our desires could bind his hands or loose his powers. Our wishes are not his commands, and faith should not be so ill-defined to imply as much. Real faith places utmost trust in God's plan and purpose. Let us not trust in what *we* decide is right, but trust that God in his love knows and will do what is right—in his time and in his way, and according to his wisdom.

The message here is that we are not responsible for directing God's will! Rather, in any situation, we are asked only to do God's will and trust him to take care of the rest. This is precisely what Shadrach, Meshach, and Abednego did. Since they did not pretend to know what would happen to them and certainly had no desire to be burned alive, they probably prayed for deliverance. Still, they recognized that their chief duty was obedience. Had they been in charge, no doubt they would have had the golden image destroyed, made Nebuchadnezzar rescind his edict, doused the furnace fires, or caused any number of other things that would keep safe their lives. None of these other things happened, and they stood on the brink of the furnace ready to die if that was God's will. They understood merely that God would use obedience for *his* purpose, not theirs.

Faith Is Not Trust in Our Ability to Read God's Will

Shadrach, Meshach, and Abednego teach us that believers are not more "holy" because they have a certainty such-and-such will happen or believe they have identified correctly what God needs to do next. The account of these faithful men crystalizes the related truth that believers are not more "faithful" when they think they can tell what God will do next. Too often Christians try to prove their faith to themselves or others by predicting God's actions. Some believers link their faith to their ability to read circumstances through the filter of providential insight. Faith of this sort is measured by the conviction with which one speaks about how

"God will bless" and by the specificity with which the blessing is described.

I once attended a prayer meeting in which a woman praised God because he was going to heal her dog. She said she knew God would do that because the very day the pet got sick she "just happened" to read in the Psalms that the Lord "heals all your diseases" (Ps. 103:3). This could be nothing less than God's "providential leading," she announced, a way to let her know what he would do.

This well-meaning but poorly informed woman had tied her faith to her ability to read circumstances in order to determine how God would act. Unfortunately, the circumstances were about to change. When we next met, this same woman told the group that her husband had experienced a heart attack during the week since our last meeting. "Obviously," she surmised, "God was not telling me that he would heal my dog when I read that psalm. God was telling me ahead of time that he would heal my husband." My first impulse, I am ashamed to admit, was to laugh inwardly. What if her son got sick the next day? What would God be saying then? What if she read, "I will strike them down with a plague," in Numbers 14:12, tomorrow? Then I remembered how often I have heard similar, if not so naive, expressions of faith from far more mature believers.

I once stayed overnight at the home of a friend when a freak snowstorm forced me to forgo a trip to my home during a college break. I stayed up late into the night with this family as they awaited the arrival of a daughter from another college. When she was many hours overdue, the unspoken worry on every mind was that she had an accident in the storm. Someone finally said, "I hope she's all right." The immediate reply from the mother was, "Of course she's all right. I have faith in God and know she'll get here safely." But the daughter never did arrive that night. She did have an accident.

Well-meaning church elders say to their pastors, "Because you are God's messenger for us and because God wants his message to go out effectively, we have prayed that God will bless your ministry. We know that whatever you propose will succeed."

Zealous and committed pastors say to their churches, "Because there is the need for an expanded gospel witness in this community and because God wants the community to hear the gospel, I know that God will provide the money we need for this building program [or this broadcasting ministry, this youth outreach, whatever]." But all kinds of projects supported with such confidence fail. The reason is that we can never really know what God's intention is. Misplaced confidence damages faith more than it accomplishes anything worthwhile.

Damage results because people believe that the mark of faith is stating in unequivocal terms what God will do in specific circumstances. Faith remains strong as long as the "reading" of circumstances seems correct and the projects succeed as expected. But should the reading prove mistaken or the human idea of "progress" not be attained, faith itself staggers. Again, the problem is an unbiblical definition of faith. Circumstances are not a means by which we can predetermine God's will or judge his purposes.

If prior knowledge of outcomes is what determines the quality of one's faith, Shadrach, Meshach, and Abednego missed the mark. Not one of them claimed to know for certain that they would not be burned alive. They were not concerned about being able to read the future. They were only concerned about responding correctly to the present circumstances. Regardless of what the king would do to them, they would obey God.

These men of faith defined faith as a righteous commitment to *do* God's will, rather than as a mystical ability to *read* God's mind. They did not tie their faith to expectations, but submitted their circumstances and their actions to God, in the faith that he would act appropriately. The three were not out to second-guess God. Their faith was marked solely by faithful obedience amidst those circumstances. This was a faith that accurately comprehended the tasks assigned by God to the faithful. God expects us to act in accord with his Word as we trust him to work in accord with his perfect will. If our faith is in God's greater purposes, it will not fluctuate with changing circumstances or unexpected results.

One group of believers who exemplify this kind of trust is the North African Mission. This agency has dedicated itself to reaching Muslims with the gospel of Jesus Christ for most of this century. Yet only in recent years has the mission experienced any real success. Although now their impact is mushrooming in the Third World, in 1934, after a generation of witnessing, the ministry counted more deaths among missionaries and their children than it could count conversions. What if someone had then equated faith with circumstances or short-term expectations?

Immediate circumstances can never be trusted to indicate with certainty what our actions should be or what God's purposes are. The wisest king who ever lived wrote about the futility of trying to determine God's will on that basis. Solomon said,

> There is something else meaningless that occurs on earth: righteous men who get what the wicked deserve, and wicked men who get what the righteous deserve. . . . No one can comprehend what goes on under the sun. Despite all his efforts to search it out, man cannot discover its meaning. Even if a wise man claims he knows, he cannot really comprehend it. So I reflected on all this and concluded that the righteous and the wise and what they do are in God's hands, but no man knows if love or hate awaits him [Eccles. 8:14–9:1].

If your faith depends on determining what circumstances mean, you will be involved in a futile religion. But if faith means trusting God enough to obey him despite *apparently* futile circumstances, God can work mightily through you. It follows that you do not have to know what will happen or why something already did. With a strong, vibrant faith, you can say with words and action, "My faith is so great that I trust God in whatever happens. As long as I do his will, I am in his care. That is sufficient for me."

Great faith does not claim to know what only God can know; it claims only to know the God who knows. This can be a message of great comfort to many believers. It means we need not trust in special divinations, so-called revelations, or expressions of sanctified optimism in order to be "faithful." We are not lesser Christians because others claim they know more about what our circumstances mean. We can be content to trust and obey, just like Shadrach, Meshach, and Abednego, whose simple, obedient faith held them in God's care through a fiery furnace. If other Christians turn to a faith that is merely confidence in personal desires and general optimism, we will search for something deeper and more solid. Biblical faith is not the stuff dreams are made of. Real faith is tougher, more resilient, more aware of the complexities of a fallen world, and more trusting of a sovereign God who loves us.

Faith Is Trust in God Alone

By their example, Shadrach, Meshach, and Abednego lay out a simple plan of action to help us faithfully confront the trials we face:

1. We acknowledge our needs without stipulating how God must respond or will respond.
2. We acknowledge and confess the ability of God to meet our needs in *either* the way we desire *or* in a way he knows is better.
3. We commit ourselves to uncompromising obedience, however uncertain or unrewarding may seem the immediate situation. We simply obey God and trust him to take care of the circumstances.

". . . he rewards those who earnestly seek him" (Heb. 11:6). The rewards may not be what we expect, nor come as we anticipate, but faith understands the perfection of God's plan and trusts the love that prepares it so carefully.

Faith that honors God above our own desires is not mere fatalism. We are not to shrug our shoulders and say, "What will be, will be." The reason we trust God, seek him, and pray to him is that he has demonstrated his love for us. When Shadrach, Meshach, and Abednego were cast into the furnace, another appeared with them. Three men were cast in, but Nebuchadnezzar saw four in the fire—and the fourth looked divine (3:25). Nebuchadnezzar did not understand. We do! The very presence of God was with the three believers. God delivered them, though there were flames all about. The same God who delivered these three delivers us. In the person of his Son, God came to be with us, endured the trials of this world, and suffered to deliver us from the flames of hell forever. Now we trust this God, knowing he always has our best interests in mind (Rom. 8:28–32). He is our Father. Why should we not trust his provision if we know his nature is loving and good? He proves his love by the cross of Jesus. Our faith now rests in that love. When our optimism has dried up, or we are not certain what the best turn of events might be, we can still rest in God's love. Although we are unable to predict how God will handle a situation, we can still rest in his love. Because the God who is all-powerful and all-wise has shown how much he cares for us through the cross of Jesus Christ, faith abides in our hearts, even when our minds cannot search out his reasons. We trust him because of his love.

While I was pastoring a rural church in which farmers and coal miners—people accustomed to hard lives—predominated the congregation, I heard a story that taught me much about the nature and foundation of true faith. There was once a miner who, though a stalwart believer, was injured in the mines at a young age. He became an invalid and over the years watched through a window beside his bed as life passed him by. He watched men of his own age prosper, raise families, and have grandchildren. He watched, but he did not share the rewards or the joys of others with whom he had once worked. As he watched, his body withered, his house crumbled, and his life wasted away.

One day, when the bedridden miner was quite old, a younger man came to visit him. "I hear that you believe in God and claim that he loves you," said the young man. "How can you believe such things after what has happened to you? Don't you sometimes doubt God's love?"

The old man hesitated and then smiled. He said, "Yes, it is true. Sometimes Satan comes calling on me in this fallen-down old house of mine. He sits right there by my bed where you are sitting now. He points out my window to the men I once worked with who are still strong and active, and Satan asks, 'Does Jesus love you?' Then Satan casts a jeering glance around my tattered room as he points to the fine homes of my friends across the street and asks again, 'Does Jesus love you?' Then, at last, Satan points to the grandchild of a friend of mine—a man who has everything I do not—and Satan waits for the tear in my eye before he whispers in my ear, 'Does Jesus really love you?' "

"And what do you say when Satan speaks to you that way?" asked the young man.

Said the old miner, "I take Satan by the hand. I lead him in my mind to a hill far away called Calvary. There I point to the thorn-tortured brow, to the nail-pierced hands and feet, and to the spear-wounded side. Then I ask Satan, 'Doesn't Jesus love me?' "

The cross is the warrant for confidence in God, despite lifelong heartache. Had any of us stood at the foot of the cross and seen the horror, we might have cried out to God to stop the suffering. But God knew better. He did not stop it till the life of the One who hung there had bled away. The agony did not mean that God failed, nor that the faith of the One who died was weak. In the suffering was a purpose so loving, so powerful, and so good that our eternity changed as a result—our sins were washed away. When our focus remains on the cross, our faith will not waver though troubles come and human answers fail. Such faith does not depend on emotional intensity, on knowing what should happen, or on a certainty of what God will do. True biblical faith acknowledges that God knows all and is doing what is right—because he loves us so much.

4

"Me with You"

(Daniel 4)

The Word

Let your imagination run wild for a few moments and imagine that you and the streets of your hometown have been transported to ancient Babylon. The streets bustle with activity that is familiar to you and are crowded with the people you know. But ahead of you a block or so you see a now uncommon sight: a man handing out religious tracts. The activity arouses your interest since you like to see what others believe and teach about God. You walk toward the tract peddler and reach out a hand to take one of his pamphlets. Then, just as the tract brushes your fingertips, you see the face of the tract peddler.

You recoil in horror at the face. It is King Nebuchadnezzar! Not only are you shocked that the king is among his subjects, but you are amazed that a man like Nebuchadnezzar would choose to publish anything about God. This is the despicably cruel ruler of Babylon, the king who captured and exiled God's chosen people. He has always enforced his whims by lopping off the heads of his subjects and even issued death decrees for scores of his advisers simply because they could not interpret dreams he would not describe. You know he has created idols for worship and ordered the live cremation of all who object to worshiping them. Surely this is no man to tell others of the Lord.

Should you take the evangelistic tract from the hand of

Nebuchadnezzar? As odd as it may seem, I suggest you do. That tract is the portion of the Book of Daniel that is now before you.

Chapter four of Daniel is Nebuchadnezzar's message for anyone who needs to know that God can perform miracles in hearts hardened against him. Look at the opening verses, which show that God did an amazing heart-changing work in Nebuchadnezzar's life. God demonstrated rewards are available for all who will seek him, regardless of sinful pasts. Now Nebuchadnezzar tells of God's amazing work despite his wicked past. In this poignant account of a man's ruin and restoration, the king not only reviews the rewards of those who stand *with* God but also reveals God's mercy toward those who have previously stood against him. Nebuchadnezzar's account is a timeless reminder that God honors those who take a stand for him today, even if they failed to do so yesterday.

1 ***King Nebuchadnezzar,***

To the peoples, nations and men of every language, who live in all the world:

May you prosper greatly!

2 ***It is my pleasure to tell you about the miraculous signs and wonders that the Most High God has performed for me.***

3 *How great are his signs,*
how mighty his wonders!
His kingdom is an eternal kingdom;
his dominion endures from generation to generation.

4 I, Nebuchadnezzar, was at home in my palace, contented
and prosperous. 5 I had a dream that made me afraid. As I was
lying in my bed, the images and visions that passed through
my mind terrified me. 6 So I commanded that all the wise men
of Babylon be brought before me to interpret the dream for
me. 7 When the magicians, enchanters, astrologers and divin-
ers came, I told them the dream, but they could not interpret
it for me. 8 Finally, Daniel came into my presence and I told
him the dream. (He is called Belteshazzar, after the name of
my god, and the spirit of the holy gods is in him.)

[9]I said, "Belteshazzar, chief of the magicians, I know that
the spirit of the holy gods is in you, and no mystery is too
difficult for you. Here is my dream; interpret it for me. [10]These
are the visions I saw while lying in my bed: I looked, and there
before me stood a tree in the middle of the land. Its height
was enormous. [11]The tree grew large and strong and its top
touched the sky; it was visible to the ends of the earth. [12]Its
leaves were beautiful, its fruit abundant, and on it was food
for all. Under it the beasts of the field found shelter, and the
birds of the air lived in its branches; from it every creature
was fed.

[13]"In the visions I saw while lying in my bed, I looked, and
there before me was a messenger, a holy one, coming down
from heaven. [14]He called in a loud voice: 'Cut down the tree
and trim off its branches; strip off its leaves and scatter its
fruit. Let the animals flee from under it and the birds from
its branches. [15]But let the stump and its roots, bound with
iron and bronze, remain in the ground, in the grass of the
field.

" 'Let him be drenched with the dew of heaven, and let him
live with the animals among the plants of the earth. [16]Let his
mind be changed from that of a man and let him be given the
mind of an animal, till seven times pass by for him.

[17]***" 'The decision is announced by messengers, the holy
ones declare the verdict, so that the living may know that
the Most High is sovereign over the kingdoms of men and
gives them to anyone he wishes and sets over them the
lowliest of men.'***

[18]"This is the dream that I, King Nebuchadnezzar, had.
Now, Belteshazzar, tell me what it means, for none of the wise
men in my kingdom can interpret it for me. But you can,
because the spirit of the holy gods is in you."

[19]Then Daniel (also called Belteshazzar) was greatly per-
plexed for a time, and his thoughts terrified him. So the king
said, "Belteshazzar, do not let the dream or its meaning alarm
you."

Belteshazzar answered, "My lord, if only the dream applied
to your enemies and its meaning to your adversaries! [20]The
tree you saw, which grew large and strong, with its top touch-
ing the sky, visible to the whole earth, [21]with beautiful leaves
and abundant fruit, providing food for all, giving shelter to

the beasts of the field, and having nesting places in its
branches for the birds of the air—[22]you, O king, are that tree!
You have become great and strong; your greatness has grown
until it reaches the sky, and your dominion extends to distant
parts of the earth.

[23]"You, O king, saw a messenger, a holy one, coming down
from heaven and saying, 'Cut down the tree and destroy it,
but leave the stump, bound with iron and bronze, in the grass
of the field, while its roots remain in the ground. Let him be
drenched with the dew of heaven; let him live like the wild
animals, until seven times pass by for him.'

[24]"This is the interpretation, O king, and this is the decree
the Most High has issued against my lord the king: [25]You will
be driven away from people and will live with the wild animals;
you will eat grass like cattle and be drenched with the dew of
heaven. Seven times will pass by for you until you acknowl-
edge that the Most High is sovereign over the kingdoms of
men and gives them to anyone he wishes. [26]The command to
leave the stump of the tree with its roots means that your
kingdom will be restored to you when you acknowledge that
Heaven rules. [27]Therefore, O king, be pleased to accept my
advice: Renounce your sins by doing what is right, and your
wickedness by being kind to the oppressed. It may be that
then your prosperity will continue."

[28]All this happened to King Nebuchadnezzar. [29]Twelve
months later, as the king was walking on the roof of the royal
palace of Babylon, [30]***he said, "Is not this the great Babylon***
I have built as the royal residence, by my mighty power
and for the glory of my majesty?"

[31]The words were still on his lips when a voice came from
heaven, "This is what is decreed for you, King Nebuchadnez-
zar: Your royal authority has been taken from you. [32]You will
be driven away from people and will live with the wild animals;
you will eat grass like cattle. Seven times will pass by for you
until you acknowledge that the Most High is sovereign over
the kingdoms of men and gives them to anyone he wishes."

[33]Immediately what had been said about Nebuchadnezzar
was fulfilled. He was driven away from people and ate grass
like cattle. His body was drenched with the dew of heaven

until his hair grew like the feathers of an eagle and his nails like the claws of a bird.

34 ***At the end of that time, I, Nebuchadnezzar, raised my eyes toward heaven, and my sanity was restored. Then I praised the Most High; I honored and glorified him who lives forever.***

His dominion is an eternal dominion;
his kingdom endures from generation to generation.
35 ***All the people of the earth are regarded as nothing.***
He does as he pleases
with the powers of heaven
and the peoples of the earth.
No one can hold back his hand
or say to him: "What have you done?"

36 At the same time that my sanity was restored, my honor and splendor were returned to me for the glory of my kingdom. My advisers and nobles sought me out, and I was restored to my throne and became even greater than before.
37 *Now I, Nebuchadnezzar, praise and exalt and glorify the King of Heaven, because everything he does is right and all his ways are just. And those who walk in pride he is able to humble.*

Daniel 4 (*Emphasis added*)

A Shattered Colossus

The poet Percy Bysshe Shelley tells of meeting "a traveler from an antique land" who describes the ruins of a great statue in the desert. The head, half sunk in the sand, lies apart from vast stone legs still on their pedestal. The shattered face is not so disfigured, though, that it does not yet portray a sneer of royal arrogance and imperial contempt. The words on the statue's pedestal confirm the look on the face:

> "My name is Ozymandias, King of Kings:
> Look on my works, ye mighty, and despair!"

But, beyond these words and these relics, the poet relates:

> Nothing beside remains. Round the decay
> Of that colossal wreck, boundless and bare
> The lone and level sands stretch far away.

The words of Shelley's fabled Ozymandias echo in Nebuchadnezzar's prideful claims in this fourth chapter of Daniel. Like the king in Shelley's poem, Babylon's ruler forgot that time and circumstance erode all the accomplishments of men, making pride absurd. Thirty-two years had passed since Daniel's first dream interpretation burst Nebuchadnezzar's illusions about his greatness (2:36–46). It seems that now Nebuchadnezzar needed a reminder. He had obviously again convinced himself that nothing could challenge *his* achievements and *his* glory. He walked atop his palace, surveyed his kingdom, and said, "Is this not the great Babylon *I* have built as the royal residence, by *my* mighty power and for the glory of *my* majesty" (4:30). The king was asking for trouble. And that is exactly what he got.

God had Nebuchadnezzar dream of a majestic tree, growing to wondrous heights only to be cut down and stripped of its branches at the command of a heavenly messenger. The stump remained, though bound with metal bands and drenched with dew. Without further explanation, the mysterious messenger said, "Let *him* be drenched with dew like an animal in the fields, and let *him* have the mind of an animal for seven years, so that all the living will know only the Most High is truly king" (4:15b–17, paraphrased).

The dream so terrified the king that he again called for Daniel to interpret the vision. The interpretation was as simple as it was alarming. King Nebuchadnezzar was going to have a great fall. He was going to become psychotic, would believe himself to be an animal, and would live in the fields until he acknowledged that only God is sovereign of all. But this is only the surface meaning of Nebuchadnezzar's dream. The question still remains as to what *we* are supposed to learn from the experiences of an ancient, pagan king. Note that the chapter opens with the promise that there will be a message for "the peoples, nations and men of every language who live in all the world." What is here for us in the fourth chapter of Daniel?

The answer is repeated three times in the chapter, but verse 17 says it best: the account is written, ". . . so that the living may know that the Most High is sovereign over the kingdoms of men and gives them to anyone he wishes and sets over them the lowliest of men." All three clauses of this key verse contain an essential truth that God intends for us to glean from the king's testimony. As such, the verse beautifully organizes God's message of love and hope.

God Is in Charge of What Man Cannot Control

The heavenly verdict was rendered, first, so all humanity would realize that "the Most High is sovereign over the kingdoms of men." The word *sovereign* pertains to the supreme power of a ruler, king, or lord. Nebuchadnezzar had begun to believe himself to be in absolute control of his realm and destiny. God reminded him in no uncertain terms that there is only one true authority over the dominions of men: the King of kings. Through his dealings with Nebuchadnezzar, God tells us always to remember that he is in control, and we are not.

Human smarts, abilities, and accomplishments are not what determine our futures or even provide our security. From a heavenly perspective, we have little or no control over what will ultimately happen to us. This would be a difficult truth for a proud and powerful man like Nebuchadnezzar to accept, but it is little easier for most of us to admit either. In our "John Wayne" culture, where independence and self-reliance are highly prized, there is no more difficult a truth to communicate than our total dependence on God. We want to be self-made men and women. We want "freedom"—self-sufficiency, autonomy, and control over circumstances.

From our youngest years we are taught to take charge of our own lives, to make our own "good luck." Study longer, work harder, plan better than the next guy—that is how to succeed. We fall for the line that those who strive for excellence hold their future in their own hands.

Do not misunderstand me. There is nothing wrong with aiming high, and God expects us to make full and diligent use of the gracius gifts he has given us. But we are to remember they are gifts. Talent, brains, and opportunity mean nothing apart from God's working. If you begin to trust only what *you* can do, to believe that *you* are the sole cause of your success, life will begin to whisper how foolish is your "faith."

From the time my parents were married until I was married and having children, my father worked for only one company as a highly skilled farm manager. Dad turns failing farms into profitable ones or manages farms for absent landowners. He is without question one of the smartest, hardest-working, most honest men I have ever known. (I do not mind bragging about my father!) He climbed the ranks in his company from being an insignificant feature writer for their agricultural magazine, to becoming the editor of that magazine, until he eventually assumed charge of all public relations for the firm. Later Dad tried his hand at agricultural sales and management and quickly became tops at that, too, winning first-place awards year after year. He became a department head and finally a regional manager. For thirty years, my father excelled as a valuable employee, secure in his company.

Then the firm's owner retired and sold his company to a large conglomerate. For unclear reasons, which probably involved tax write-offs, this corporation sold off the more profitable divisions of the company and seemed almost purposefully to mismanage what remained. My father received orders to manage his region in ways he knew were unwise. The regional office became a shambles, but his suggestions to the corporate office went unheeded. When the region ceased providing a profit, the corporation decided to get rid of that arm of the company. So, after thirty years of service and achievement, my father was without a job. Decisions over which he had no control had stolen his security.

My father is an intelligent, resourceful man, so he offered to take the "unprofitable" region off the corporation's hands to manage it his own way. They agreed, and he set up his own company. The operation quickly turned a profit. In one year my father made more money than he had ever made before.

One reason for this near-instant success was that my father's independent company assumed exclusive management rights to a huge farming operation near Springhill, Tennessee. The name of this small Tennessee town may sound familiar, since at this moment General Motors is conducting a multimillion-dollar experiment in automotive production there. GM is constructing the Saturn plant in Springhill to introduce a new concept in automotive production and marketing to America. Guess which tract of land GM purchased for that plant? That's right! They chose the farm that had become the backbone of my father's new business. For the second time in five years my father (who had had security and success for the previous thirty) was damaged by forces over which he had no control. He is no less intelligent, able, or hard-working than he ever was, but he realizes—as all in our family realize more than before—that no one is truly in charge of his own destiny. There are forces larger, more complex, and more hidden than any man of whatever caliber can control. As much as we may want it otherwise, and as often as we may think otherwise, we are not ultimately in charge. Only God is sovereign. Man's "control" is flawed in three basic ways:

Man's Power Is Fragile

God uses the experience of Nebuchadnezzar to declare the unreliability of all the human means that men use to assert their sovereignty. As the king attempted to use power, wisdom, and accomplishment as a hedge against the insecurity that faces any human, God rebuked every attempt. Men can never know enough, do enough, or have enough to control their own lives. Nebuchadnezzar thought his great power and abilities made him sovereign, and he said so (4:30). He forgot how fragile are all the trappings of human greatness. In twelve months this king slid from his power over the worlds' greatest dominion and became a pathetic figure lacking control of even his own faculties. God merely stirred Nebuchadnezzar's thoughts to show how fragile the position of the world's most powerful ruler was. A mental disease convinced the king he was a wild animal, proving that the greatest of human powers is more fragile than we often dare to consider.

Not only can small changes in our minds result in big changes in our lives, but small—even minute—changes in how our bodies work can do the same. The St. Louis Cardinals baseball team currently has a promising young infielder. He has a great glove, but last season his batting average was terrible. It seemed as if everyone wanted to trade him, according to radio talk shows that had him branded as a loser. This year, though, was different. This same infielder nearly led the league in hitting, so he is now considered one of the key members of the team, a hero. This season the call-in shows talk only about how great he is. Do you know what is the difference for this young man between being great and being a loser? It's much less than you might guess. Last year, only a little more than two out of every ten times he walked to the plate did he get a hit. That was awful. How much better did he have to do this year to be considered a winner? He got a hit slightly fewer than three out of every ten times he went to the plate this year. That labeled him "great." A margin of difference of less than one in every ten attempts separated awful from great! Is not greatness based on human ability the most fragile of commodities?

Man's Wisdom Is Limited

Perhaps it is not physical strength or personal ability that you depend on to control situations. You may be wise enough to see the fragility and temporality of this kind of power. But that very wisdom is what many believe grants them security. Do you believe yourself smart enough to handle whatever comes your way? Nebuchadnezzar surrounded himself with the wise and learned so that expert advice was available for all contingencies. His "security" at least partially rested upon human intelligence and acquired knowledge. The problem is that such wisdom always has its limits. Nebuchadnezzar's wisemen could not answer all his questions, nor can today's experts answer ours.

Investors spend millions yearly getting so-called expert market analyses. Yet how many of them were prepared for the financial markets' collapse of October 1987? On that Black Monday the Dow Jones Industrial Average dove an unprecedented 508 points. In the course of just six hours, one publication reported, the richest man in the United States lost several billion dollars. For several decades that man had used his business and financial acumen (and those of his advisers) to earn those billions, and in half a day half of his fortune was gone. Of course, since that Black Monday, the stockmarket has rebounded, and some of that billionaire's lost billions are back in his financial holdings. The point is that neither the loss of those billions nor their later return resulted from anything the billionaire could control. He was just a spectator at the mercy of forces that could again turn mean.

Those of us who are not at such pinnacles of wealth nevertheless face the same financial insecurities. Recently my employer asked the staff to make some decisions about how we individually wanted to invest our retirement funds. I asked this expert and that expert and a third. I found that everyone has advice on how to secure your future, but no one really knows. Oh, the real estate people tell you to invest in a house, but no one really knows if this advice applies in a particular situation or location. I know those who have invested their life's savings in a home, only to have a local economy go bad. Then their house value plummets and potential profits evaporate. Others discover a structural flaw that previously went undetected and will cost thousands to repair. The foundation shifts; the highway gets re-routed; radon gas creeps in; city fathers rezone or put a prison next door or a dump across the street; the airport routes a new flight path over your roof. No one can plan for all the contingencies. We try to do the best we can with what we know, but we realize we can never know enough. The truly wise know there is no security in human wisdom, since no one can prepare for all the possibilities.

Human Accomplishment Is Always in Jeopardy

When most of us consider the fragility of our abilities and the limitations of our wisdom, our response is to do what we can to beat the odds. We resolve to "get while the getting is good." Since nothing man does is secure forever, we do what we can to prepare for hard times by massing up enough of this world's goods and favors as protection against incidental setbacks. We begin to look for security in worldly treasures and accomplishments. Like Nebuchadnezzar, we may survey all we have been able to build to give us assurance of our security (Dan. 4:30). The trouble is, no one can ever amass enough material protection from all life's vagaries. A famous basketball player recently signed a multimillion-dollar contract at age forty so he could keep playing for two more years. The sports analysts shook their heads. Surely, with all his years of superstar salary, this player was secure enough to retire. As it turned out, though, the pro-athlete had just lost $10 million in bad investments. He learned what we all know deep down inside: you can never have enough to make you completely secure.

Yet, even in the church, our actions contradict what we really know about "security." Even as we heap up assets for ourselves, the basic insecurity of human existence is always jeopardizing our positions, power, and wealth. So the more we accumulate, the more frantically we try to hold on to our possessions. The bricks of accomplishment we use to build a wall against failure are forever taking on the appearance of marbles threatening to roll away. We keep trying to add more and more marbles to the pile so the ones that get away will not matter so much. But it never works. Marbles piled higher only threaten to roll further away.

Wealth has a strange effect—even on Christians. As strange as it may seem, the wealthier a Christian becomes, the less likely he is to give sacrificially to God's work and the more likely he is to cling to the wealth he does have. Internal Revenue Service statistics released a few years ago indicate that church members who earned $15,000 or less per year gave an average of 6 percent of their income to the church. At the same time, members who earned $50,000 or more gave less than 1 percent. The overall average giving percentage for believers in this most affluent nation the world has ever known is 2.5 percent. It seems the greater our accomplishments total, the more tightly we hold to them. We apparently do not feel more secure when we stand high on the success ladder; we simply fear we have further to fall if things go wrong. So we cling to what we have, though we have already lost our confidence in the security it provides. Our own actions indicate we know climbing higher does not make us more secure.

My family recently attended a church camp in Colorado. During the trip we visited a stone castle that a man with a peculiar but spectacular vision is building by himself in the Rockies. The castle has huge stone turrets, with winding staircases leading to a breathtaking but precarious mountaintop view. As my two young sons started climbing with me up the stairs, which had no bannisters, they ignored my fatherly cautions. I had to rather sternly remind them to hold my hands. The higher we climbed, the less of a reminder they needed. By the time we reached the top I felt as if my hands were being crunched inside two miniature vises. The boys clung to my hands with far more fervor than when we were on the lower steps. Even children know that being high up makes you less secure because you have further to fall. Adults confess that feeling in the way we cling to our wealth. There is no more security to be found in material stockpiles, than there is in human wisdom or power. The things for which we strive to make us more secure, once achieved, only make our situations more perilous.

By examining the flaws in man's efforts to control his life, you probably see that we can be more like Nebuchadnezzar than it is pleasant to confess. If our abilities or hard work have apparently brought us success, we can easily believe our security is solely the product of *our* efforts. Like Nebuchadnezzar, you may scan what you have built—whether it be in terms of academic, commercial, professional, or church accomplishment—and think how great you are. You've done it! Maybe you did, but not alone. Think of how the events behind your successes simply "fell into place." Remember how you were "in the right place at the right time." Imagine how a different person here or a different circumstance there could have changed the results. Think about family members, classmates, or professional peers. Perhaps their lives are dreary, though they are just as smart or smarter than you, just as capable, just as industrious. Now ask yourself whether *you* made all the difference. Is everything you have because of your own doing? It is difficult to confess that we are not really in charge of our lives, but it is a confession that God and conscience require.

God Grants What Man Cannot Earn

Nebuchadnezzar's testimony contains a second major lesson. Not only does he remind us that God alone is in ultimate control, but he teaches us that it is up to God to *grant* what we cannot gain on our own. When we begin to see that human power, wisdom, and accomplishment alone cannot account for worldly success, a typical response might be to look for something else in ourselves that will justify God's blessing. But that means we still want control. We still want the touchstone of success to be in *our* hands! A particular temptation for Christians is to link success with "goodness." If we have accomplished anything at all, we may believe this is because we are morally or spiritually superior to others. You reason, "Surely God must find me worthy. My righteousness has been rewarded." But God answers, "Not by might nor by power but by my Spirit . . ." (Zech. 4:6). The seventeenth verse of Daniel 4 continues this theme: ". . . the Most High is sovereign over the kingdoms of men *and gives them to anyone he wishes. . . .*" (italics mine). God not only proclaims himself sovereign, the only one in charge. He says that he grants kingdoms to whomever he wills. There is no human factor. God provides as he determines best.

An honest assessment of your life in comparison to those around you probably reveals how insignificant human "goodness" figures in success. If you have accomplished anything, it requires very little reflection to recall worse people who have done far better—and better people who have done far worse. If you hold up your righteous works before God and say, "For these I am blessed," you speak foolishness. The Scriptures say that even our best works, with their mix of human motives and frailties, are only "filthy rags" to God (Isa. 64:6). When we have dutifully done everything we should do as mere humans, we are still unworthy servants of God (Luke 17:10).

How foolish to claim that the reason we have anything is because of our moral superiority! And who would laugh the loudest if we made such a claim? Nebuchadnezzar. He was the richest, most powerful man of his time—king of earth's kings. But was he on top because he was morally good? Hardly. He was a wicked, cruel, vindictive man and probably knew it. There was very little correlation between goodness and success in Nebuchadnezzar's life. If there was any link, it was an inverse relationship. When men count their accomplishments, they cannot claim goodness as the cause. This was true of Nebuchadnezzar and just as true of us. If we have anything to boast about, let us never believe it is because of our goodness. Solely for *his* purposes, God *chooses* to bless us with his provision. The only secret to success is grace—and grace alone. Our gain is simply what God grants.

Grace lies behind both secular accomplishments and spiritual victories. There is evidence in this passage of God's granting Nebuchadnezzar more than an earthly kingdom. By the end of his testimony, this king praises, exalts, and glorifies "the King of heaven" (4:37). If Nebuchadnezzar reaps the benefits of the kingdom of God, a pagan king is thereby granted rights to spiritual eternity. Why did God reach down to touch Nebuchadnezzar's heart and turn him toward heaven? Was the king morally better than his subjects? Had he done more good? No, definitely not! Spiritually, Nebuchadnezzar was a wretched nothing. Nothing this man had done earned God's grace.

This truth, God's absolute mercy to those who have nothing good in themselves, is a central feature of this message from Daniel. Despite our sin and guilt, God makes us members of the ruling family of his kingdom simply because he loves us. He grants the kingdom's gifts to whomever he wills. Because no one is worthy or deserving of God's kingdom in light of God's absolute holiness, this is a truth we all desperately need to hear. If we are anything before God, it is because of his grace alone, not because of any worthiness in us. This may not be a truth we want to hear on our good days, but it is a truth we *must* hear on our bad days, when our spiritual health may depend on whether we remember this grace.

Some time ago a young man who had struggled with life-threatening depression years earlier phoned, asking to visit me. For much of his life my young Christian friend had wrestled with a particular kind of immorality that much of society now blithely approves, but which can capture and twist one's personality. By diligently seeking God's instruction and grace, however, Bill (as I'll call him) had seemed to gain victory over his sinful lifestyle. Now he wanted to see me again, and I could tell from his tone of voice on the phone that there was a problem.

Bill told me the story as soon as he arrived. After much accomplishment, the young man had lately experienced some financial and family setbacks. His once-successful business began to fail, and his family life deteriorated with the increased pressure. As his world seemed to be collapsing, the pressures became so continuous, so intense, that my friend felt he had to find some relief. So he sought escape in his old lifestyle. In a moment of great agony and weakness, he fell hard and deep into the old perversity. This time the sin seemed even worse because of his abandonment of the victory the Lord had previously provided. He confessed it all with great grief and many tears, although without the despair I anticipated. The man for whose life I had wrestled could now tell of his greatest failure without the hopeless words that once made me fear for his safety.

The reason for Bill's newfound strength was soon explained. Following the agony of the confession came his words of amazement. With wonder in his voice, Bill explained that since his sinful relapse, he had felt the presence of God more closely than ever. In fact, he had found the sin so foreign to his new nature that now he knew he was free from its grip for the first time in his adult life. This young man's circumstances were now improving on all fronts. He had a new job, which had led him to a new home away from past temptations. As financial pressures eased, family relationships were healing. He explained that he was even able to relate to people at church in a way he previously could not fathom.

My friend's self-image, his business, his family life, even

his worship, had all miraculously improved from the moment of what he considered the worst sin of his life. He was amazed. "Bryan," he said, "it's not supposed to work this way, is it? I betrayed you and all you tried to do for me. Even worse, I failed God. I denied him and his victory in my life. Though I must have hurt him terribly, all he is doing now is blessing me, and blessing me, and blessing me. How can this be? I surely don't deserve it."

I had the privilege of telling my friend Bill what we all must learn again and again in our Christian lives: ". . . when the kindness and love of God our Savior appeared, he saved us, not because of righteous things we have done, but because of his mercy . . ." (Titus 3:4–5). God's love is not conditioned on our goodness. He does not call certain people his own because they have been better than others. God loves us simply because that is his nature. This does not mean we can sin without consequence. God will do whatever is necessary to bring his loved ones into fellowship with himself. He may use discipline, as he did with Nebuchadnezzar. Or he may use inexplicable mercy, as he did with my young friend (cf. Rom. 2:4). But whether the actions of God toward us are harsh or gentle, his motive is always love, and his provision is available by grace alone. Neither Nebuchadnezzar nor my friend nor any of us deserves God's grace, so God grants what we cannot gain on our own in the way he knows is most appropriate for each heart.

My friend, Bill, had the great privilege of knowing for certain what it takes so many Christians a lifetime to discover: God loves his children just because they *are* his, not because they have earned his favor. They never could be holy enough for God's standards. When they try to become "worthy," thinking to tie his love to their goodness, they inevitably become hard and cynical. Like children who believe their parents only love them when they behave, Christians who believe they are loved because of their righteousness grow bitter and resentful. If we believe our heavenly Father's affection is conditional, we may obey him to earn his blessing but probably we do not like him very much. We may fear his displeasure and honor his name, but our hearts are far from his. Because our assurance of God's love rests on the belief that we are morally superior to those around us, we can easily become judgmental, bigoted, suspicious of others' motives, and the cruelest of gossips. If we always compare our behavior to the faults and frailties of others to assure ourselves that God loves us, the exercise can harden us in the worst ways. By trying to stand tall on the weaknesses of others we sink into prideful self-centeredness but eventually fall prey to uncertainties and doubt as we recognize our own weaknesses.

"Bill," I had said to my friend, "you never again in your life have to worry if you have become good enough to gain or keep God's love. You know that when you sinned your worst, God blessed you the most. When you were in your deepest, darkest pit of sin, he showed you his love most clearly."

God showed his love to Nebuchadnezzar when the once-proud king was at his lowest state. It was not when Nebuchadnezzar was at the height of his power that God claimed him, but when he was a raging animal. We must always remember that grace is not applied to those who have earned it. The temptation to build a tower to God's affection is one of the oldest and most basic sins. Babel is never very far from any of us! Pride and guilt both seek to convince us that we must climb to grace, but neither speaks truth. When the king stood high and compared his accomplishments to the attainments of others, he knew nothing of God's salvation (4:30). He saw God only when he knew that apart from God he was as humble as a beast of the field. As long as Nebuchadnezzar looked down on others, he had no part of God's kingdom. Only when he was so humbled that his eyes turned up to heaven for help did God make him whole (v. 34).

The message for us is clear: we cannot save ourselves! If

our actions lead us to the depths of sin, we must not expect our own efforts to lift us up. We, too, must lift our eyes toward heaven and ask God to save us through the blood of Jesus Christ. Some of us made that decision once, but since then our lives have sunk low again. Do you fear that God has abandoned you because of your sin? That he will not love you again until you have corrected *all* your sins? If so, let God's Word rule over your feelings. Remember that you can never do enough to gain God's love. Perhaps you did not know God's love until you hit bottom. Then, in that pit of sin, you first knew the greatness of that love. Why, then, do you now believe you must climb high before God will love you again? God loves only because he delights in his children.

If we believe or act as though God's love is a result of our goodness, such an attitude creates pride during days of apparent righteousness, but leaves only pain on days of failure. If God's love were dependent on the holiness we could achieve, we would all be destined for abandonment—because we are all sinners. But we need have no such fears. God is by nature too holy and loving a parent to treat his children so poorly. The apostle Paul says that "if we are faithless, he will remain faithful, for he cannot disown himself" (2 Tim. 2:13).

God has never shared his love on the basis of either great potential or holy attainment. On the contrary, God chose Israel as his holy nation not because of its greatness, but because it was the most desperate of nations. He *loved* them (Deut. 7:6–8). God loved the apostle Paul though as "Saul" he had murdered believers (see Acts 9:1–15). God promised David the lineage of Jesus, knowing the young king would sin greatly (2 Sam. 7:11–16). So, too, did God love a cruel, pagan king named Nebuchadnezzar, when there was no earthly reason to do so. If God so greatly loved these, he can love us, too, though our sin is great. If we mistakenly think our sin destroys the love of God, we will suppose him far from us, just when we most need his support and forgiveness. We may hold him at arm's distance, but his arms are always outstretched to receive believers, no matter how great their sin.

Even when not in the depths of sin we must recognize that our "good standing" results only from God's grace. If we have accomplished anything, this is only by the grace of God. There is no cause for boasting, or pride, or self-approval, lest arrogance deprive us of the beauty of God's provision. G. K. Chesterton said, "No man's really good till he knows how bad he is, or might be." Until we recognize that any sin would be sufficient cause for God to remove his love from us, we are not properly appreciative of God. Until we understand the necessity of grace for everyone, the cross of Jesus Christ will seem distant, removed, and needed only by others.

When I see that to adorn myself in my finest robes of righteousness is still to stand in filthy rags before God, I begin to glimpse the wonder of God's love. I begin to sense the meaning of the cross for me. My ears can no longer tune out the agony of his death. My eyes can no longer blink away the sight of his blood. My heart can only live for him who died for me, undeserving though I am.

There are those, of course, who teach God's love as conditional on our righteousness, hoping that believers will be spurred on to greater holiness. Nothing could be further from the truth. Although obedience provides for the greater experiencing of God's love, mere obedience does not produce more of God's love. Whenever believers seek to earn God's affection, they focus more on their works than on his. By making good deeds the warrant for God's love rather than the result of his love, they diminish the cross and the love of the Savior. Seeking your own holiness deprives you of its one true source. Since true righteousness springs from hearts fully aware of the mercy of God, the strongest testimonies come from the most grateful people, those humbled by the realization that though they could never attain God's favor, he grants it anyway.

God Promises a Kingdom for the Lowliest

So far, Nebuchadnezzar's message in Daniel 4:17 is as humbling for us as the account is humiliating for him. Through the pagan king's fall we learn that because (1) only God is sovereign and (2) he grants his kingdom to whomever he wishes, we cannot stand proudly on our abilities or our goodness. When we have neither of these legs on which to stand, we are brought low. Nebuchadnezzar seems only to offer discouragement and shame, and you may be ready to discard his testimony. But the ancient king is not finished. He finally speaks of a reason for hope: ". . . [the Most High] sets over them [the kingdoms of men] the lowliest of men." The lowliest get the kingdom! Here is the encouragement our hearts need. No matter what a "low life" you may think you are, you are not automatically excluded from God's blessing. There is hope for the lowliest of us, no matter what.

. . . No Matter How Great the Sin

As a pastor, I wrestle as hard to convince believers they can be forgiven as I do to convince unbelievers they must be forgiven. Some have been helped simply by considering what a spiritual disaster Nebuchadnezzar was. He was cruel, arrogant, materialistic, idolatrous, an enemy of God's people. Yet God claimed his heart, once the king acknowledged his own lowliness. If God restored Nebuchadnezzar, he can restore anyone. You may not have been perfect, but you could not have sunk as low in sin as Babylon's king. You may have committed great sins, but surely no greater than those of this mass murderer. If God could reach a "low life" like Nebuchadnezzar, there is nothing that can stand between you and God's restoration except a failure to confess your lowliness.

How deeply the truth of God's love for the lowly must penetrate hearts is revealed in the testimony of a young girl named Fran. She had listened to the gospel as presented to her by a college friend. As she heard of the sacrifice of Jesus for her sins, she faced the seriousness of her condition for the first time. Fran's guilt was overwhelming her. Primarily because of her past sexual activity, she could not bear to think of approaching God. She said, "God can't love somebody like me. God *shouldn't* love me." Then the friend said, "It doesn't matter how great your sin. God's love is greater than all our sin." Suddenly Fran understood what the grace of God really meant. The "lowliest" are loved by God. It is when we confess that our sin has brought us so low and that none but God can restore us that he lifts us up.

Since this truth—that there is no sin greater than God's love—is central to our faith, with these words I am saying nothing new to any Christian. Yet, as familiar as the words are, the concept is never more remote than when we sin. In the throes of our sin we wonder if God truly *can* love us. We may question whether he *should* love us. But if we are ever to be truly whole, we must realize there is no sin we have ever committed, or could commit, that the grace of God cannot cover. Unless the truth of God's matchless forgiveness penetrates and overwhelms our hearts, we shall forever doubt him and fear our futures.

As the leaders of my church denomination gathered together for our annual conference this past year, a familiar song struck me with new poignancy. We stood together—a thousand elders—and sang "To God Be the Glory." The second verse of the song says:

> O perfect redemption, the purchase of blood!
> To every believer the promise of God;
> The vilest offender who truly believes,
> That moment from Jesus forgiveness receives.

There it is, I thought, *the truth we must always unite to sing*! We must shake the rafters and move the world with this truth: "The vilest offender who truly believes, that moment from Jesus forgiveness receives." From that second of repentance, and for all eternity, God's pardon covers the vilest of sins. We must never stop singing these words from our hearts. Sin too quickly makes grace a faint echo and forgiveness a distant hope. We can too easily despair if we ever forget to sing this promise of God. There is no sin so great that God cannot pardon it. May the truths of that song penetrate and comfort all our hearts.

. . . No Matter How Hard the Heart

Not only does Nebuchadnezzar indicate that God will forgive, no matter how great the sin, but his own history also teaches us that God can heal, no matter how hard the heart. Nebuchadnezzar had been hardened to God's truths. He had heard of Daniel's God for years but rejected the message. Do you know of such a person? Is there someone in your life who has heard the gospel of Jesus Christ time after time but never responded? This person is calloused against God's truths. And, if you really scratch deeply into your innermost heart and mind, you will admit that you doubt this person can be changed. You believe he or she will never accept the gospel. You have given up hope of seeing change and probably have even stopped praying for that person. To some extent you have even stopped caring. Whoever it is you remember in that way, take hope in knowing that God can change the hardest of hearts, as he did Nebuchadnezzar's.

A fellow instructor at my seminary told me recently how God had re-taught him the power of the gospel to change hearts. My instructor friend's great-aunt had died. A lifetime of selfish and careless living had long since hardened her to the gospel. Whenever someone tried to share the message of salvation with her, she either scoffed or flew into a rage. Her heart seemed untouchable. Since neither his aunt nor any of her immediate family accepted any "religion," my friend assumed there was no hope for her.

After the aunt's death, the family gathered at her house one day to divide her personal belongings. In one box on a bookshelf someone discovered some inspirational books. Since my colleague was the only "religious" person present, the family quickly decided that this box was part of his share. He took the books home, but they smelled so much of stale tobacco smoke and a stuffy house that he did not even want to touch them. He put the box of books in his attic and forgot about it.

A few months later, my friend went into the attic on some now-forgotten errand and stumbled on the box of books. He took one out and was amazed to discover it was a very fine devotional guide. He took other books from the box. Each was a solid book of Bible studies or devotions. While thumbing through a commentary on Ephesians, he came on a handwritten letter pressed between the pages. The letter was written by his aunt late in her life and addressed to God. She had obviously written the letter as a result of her study of God's Word. In the letter she confessed her sins and claimed Jesus Christ as her Savior. No matter how hard the heart, God can change it!

If God could bring Nebuchadnezzar to his knees, God can break the strongest self-will and win the hardest heart. So we must work and pray for the salvation of those God places in our care. The battle may be long before it is won. As this chapter begins, it has been thirty-two years since Daniel first began his testimony of God in Nebuchadnezzar's life. Apparently Daniel had developed an affection for the king in the intervening years (4:19), but still the ruler had not responded to Daniel's testimony. Another year passed between Daniel's interpretation of this dream and its fulfillment (v. 28). Seven more years ("times") passed before Nebuchadnezzar lifted his eyes to heaven (v. 32). A total of forty years passed before the king responded to the life and witness of Daniel. The message here is that we must not cease working and praying for a loved one. Never give up—no matter how hard the heart.

Forever His

A few years ago a young pastor, fresh out of seminary, was asked to visit a dying man in a Washington, D.C. hospital. A virulent bone cancer was quickly and painfully eating away the life of the patient, who was not a Christian. On the few occasions when the pastor presented the gospel, there was no spiritual response, but a friendship formed nevertheless. Through a number of visits the pastor learned that the patient was a remarkable "self-made man." He had been raised in Spain by a Christian mother who diligently taught her son the truths of faith, though he did not listen. The Franco regime had killed his father and, because Spain's official church supported Franco, the boy spurned faith in God. He fled his country as a young teenager and came to America knowing no English. The youth worked and studied hard. He eventually went to college and studied psychiatry, using it to confirm his atheism. Despite his early disadvantages, he became wealthy and successful—chairman of the psychiatry department of one of our nation's most prestigious hospitals. Then came the cancer.

In just a few months the malignancy destroyed the accomplishments of a lifetime. It devastated the man's body, once kept in top shape by miles of daily swimming. Even his mind began to deteriorate because of the advances of the disease. Finally, with his spirit broken and his body racked with pain, the man ran out of pride and became tired of his own answers. When the young pastor next visited, the despairing psychiatrist confronted him: "I have treated depression all my life, but I have no answers for what I'm going through. If your God really has some answers, please help me with the hell I am experiencing now. Give me some peace—if you can."

The young pastor could hardly begin to think of how to

respond. He hesitated, grasped for the right words, and when they did not seem to come simply stumbled ahead:

"You've gained everything a man could gain in every avenue of life. You have wealth, respect, and achievement. These may all have to be put aside before you gain this last thing you want. You have succeeded in every sphere of life except the spiritual, and to succeed there you must not follow any of the rules you have used before. You cannot conquer the spiritual world by your own efforts. You must first admit your helplessness and inability, confessing that you have nothing to stand on. To enter God's kingdom and know his peace you must not come as a self-sufficient man but as a helpless child."

Still there was no spiritual response from the dying man. Little else was said that night. The man remained silent. A few days later the bone cancer had progressed to the extent that the man's leg broke spontaneously as he lay in bed. The doctors had to operate to repair the damage, despite their patient's weakened condition. On the eve of that operation, unbeknownst to his family, the man wrote a note to the young pastor. In a labored scrawl he wrote in Spanish the words he had memorized years ago at his mother's knee: "I believe in God the Father Almighty, Maker of heaven and earth. And in Jesus Christ his only son our Lord . . ."—the words of the Apostles' Creed. The note continued in English with these words:

> Jesus, I hate all my sins. I have not served or worshiped
> you.
> Father, I know the only way to come into your Kingdom is
> by the precious blood of Jesus.
> I know you stand at the door and will answer those who
> knock.
> I now want to be your lamb,
> me with you.

The man who wrote those words never regained consciousness after his operation. His life was gone, but his soul was won. God is sovereign and does as he wills. But he can change the hardest hearts and wipe away the darkest sin. *He* must do it, for we cannot. Our God calls us to put aside all we trust, take pleasure in, or have used to make ourselves "worthwhile." He urges us to come to him as a helpless child and then promises us his kingdom forever. When we call to him, without trying to stand on our accomplishments or goodness, but humbled by his mercy for sinners like us, he responds. His voice is gentle and loving and his words echo our own ultimate desire. He says, "Me with you, child. Forever and ever you are mine. Now it will always be me with you."

5

Mene, Tekel, Peres . . .

(Daniel 5)

The Word

Chapter five of Daniel addresses the question of what might happen if someone gave a party and God crashed it. Nebuchadnezzar was no longer on the throne. A successor named Belshazzar ruled the land. One night Belshazzar hosted a great banquet when an unexpected and quite unusual guest appeared. The "visitor" was a disembodied set of fingers. In the sight of all the party revelers, the uninvited hand wrote a message on the palace wall. The king was so frightened that the blood drained from his face and his knees knocked. No one could explain the specter or interpret the message. The king's wisemen and counselors were called but were equally baffled, so the king grew more worried and pale with alarm. Then the queen remembered Daniel. "O king," she said, "do not be upset. Your predecessor, Nebuchadnezzar, called upon a man named Daniel to interpret dreams and solve riddles. This Daniel still lives in the kingdom. Ask him what the handwriting means."

Belshazzar summoned Daniel. The prophet interpreted the message, but he did not calm the king. Daniel prophesied divine judgment!

Chapter five of Daniel becomes the flip-side of the previous one. In chapter four we learn that Daniel used King Nebuchadnezzar's conversion to affirm that the repentant reap the rewards of grace, however bleak their past. Now Daniel will use King Belshazzar's sacrilege to declare that the rebellious reap the consequences of wrath, however secure their present. Thus, two equally evil kings will have demonstrated two equally vital messages: God's complete pardon for the humble and God's sure judgment for the proud.

1King Belshazzar gave a great banquet for a thousand of
his nobles and drank wine with them. 2While Belshazzar was
drinking his wine, he gave orders to bring in the gold and
silver goblets that Nebuchadnezzar his father had taken from
the temple in Jerusalem, so that the king and his nobles, his
wives and his concubines might drink from them. 3***So they
brought in the gold goblets that had been taken from the
temple of God in Jerusalem, and the king and his nobles,
his wives and his concubines drank from them.*** 4***As they
drank the wine, they praised the gods of gold and silver,
of bronze, iron, wood and stone.***

5Suddenly the fingers of a human hand appeared and
wrote on the plaster of the wall, near the lampstand in the
royal palace. The king watched the hand as it wrote. 6His face
turned pale and he was so frightened that his knees knocked
together and his legs gave way.

7The king called out for the enchanters, astrologers and
diviners to be brought and said to these wise men of Babylon,
"Whoever reads this writing and tells me what it means will
be clothed in purple and have a gold chain placed around his
neck, and he will be made the third highest ruler in the
kingdom."

8Then all the king's wise men came in, but they could not
read the writing or tell the king what it meant. 9So King Bel-
shazzar became even more terrified and his face grew more
pale. His nobles were baffled.

10The queen, hearing the voices of the king and his nobles,
came into the banquet hall. "O king, live forever!" she said.
"Don't be alarmed! Don't look so pale! 11There is a man in
your kingdom who has the spirit of the holy gods in him. In
the time of your father he was found to have insight and
intelligence and wisdom like that of the gods. King Nebu-
chadnezzar your father—your father the king, I say—

appointed him chief of the magicians, enchanters, astrolo-
gers and diviners. [12]This man Daniel, whom the king called
Belteshazzar, was found to have a keen mind and knowledge
and understanding, and also the ability to interpret dreams,
explain riddles and solve difficult problems. Call for Daniel,
and he will tell you what the writing means."

[13]So Daniel was brought before the king, and the king said
to him, "Are you Daniel, one of the exiles my father the king
brought from Judah? [14]I have heard that the spirit of the gods
is in you and that you have insight, intelligence and out-
standing wisdom. [15]The wise men and enchanters were
brought before me to read this writing and tell me what it
means, but they could not explain it. [16]Now I have heard that
you are able to give interpretations and to solve difficult prob-
lems. If you can read this writing and tell me what it means,
you will be clothed in purple and have a gold chain placed
around your neck, and you will be made the third highest
ruler in the kingdom."

[17]Then Daniel answered the king, "You may keep your gifts
for yourself and give your rewards to someone else. Neverthe-
less, I will read the writing for the king and tell him what it
means.

[18]"O king, the Most High God gave your father Nebuchad-
nezzar sovereignty and greatness and glory and splendor.
[19]Because of the high position he gave him, all the peoples
and nations and men of every language dreaded and feared
him. Those the king wanted to put to death, he put to death;
those he wanted to spare, he spared; those he wanted to pro-
mote, he promoted; and those he wanted to humble, he hum-
bled. [20]But when his heart became arrogant and hardened
with pride, he was deposed from his royal throne and stripped
of his glory. [21]He was driven away from people and given the
mind of an animal; he lived with the wild donkeys and ate
grass like cattle; and his body was drenched with the dew of
heaven, ***until he acknowledged that the Most High God is
sovereign over the kingdoms of men and sets over them
anyone he wishes.***

[22]"***But you his son, O Belshazzar, have not humbled
yourself, though you knew all this.*** [23]Instead, you have set
yourself up against the Lord of heaven. You had the goblets

from his temple brought to you, and you and your nobles, your wives and your concubines drank wine from them. You praised the gods of silver and gold, of bronze, iron, wood and stone, which cannot see or hear or understand. ***But you did not honor the God who holds in his hand your life and all your ways.*** 24***Therefore he sent the hand that wrote the inscription.***

25"This is the inscription that was written:

MENE, MENE, TEKEL, PARSIN

26"This is what these words mean:

Mene: God has numbered the days of your reign and brought it to an end.
27*Tekel*: You have been weighed on the scales and found wanting.
28*Peres*: Your kingdom is divided and given to the Medes and Persians."

29Then at Belshazzar's command, Daniel was clothed in purple, a gold chain was placed around his neck, and he was proclaimed the third highest ruler in the kingdom.

30***That very night Belshazzar, king of the Babylonians, was slain,*** 31and Darius the Mede took over the kingdom, at the age of sixty-two.

Daniel 5 (*Emphasis added*)

Truth and Consequences

Ferdinand Marcos	Ben Johnson
Baby Doc Duvalier	Pete Rose
Gary Hart	Jim and Tammy
Ivan Boesky	Gordon and Jimmy
John Belushi	You and Me?

Mene, Tekel, Peres. . . . Numbered out; weighed and found wanting; divided and cast down. Secure in the world; sinful before God. Judged!

Power, position, prestige, peer approval; wealth, wisdom, wonderful potential, amazing accomplishments and even esteem in the church—all count for nothing before an all-powerful, all-knowing, holy God who brings every dark thing to light and judges sin. The names change, the situations vary, but ignoring the truth brings bitter consequences.

Belshazzar was a powerful man, having become the undisputed sovereign of Babylonia, the empire that had dominated the ancient world for generations. Outside the walls of his capital a foreign army challenged the king's dominion, but Babylon's ruler was unperturbed because he thought he was in no danger. The Persian invader had been kept at bay outside the city gates for two and a half years. The walls of Babylon were as much as 350 feet high and 87 feet thick—impregnable to any war machine of that day. The metropolis surrounded by these mammoth walls was itself so spacious that food could be cultivated within its walls. The River Euphrates flowed right through the city, supplying a fresh and ample source of water for people, cattle, and crops. Babylon could not be starved into submission. Belshazzar felt quite secure! So confident was he of his safety that Belshazzar threw a party. By hosting a feast the king was thumbing his nose at the enemy as if to say, "You don't worry us a bit. That's because weaklings don't scare us. You want to know what I think of your siege? It's not enough to keep me from throwing the biggest bash this kingdom has ever seen."

So arrogant was Belshazzar that he even decided to thumb his nose at God, ignoring the vivid lessons God had taught his predecessor, Nebuchadnezzar. The power of Jehovah of Israel and the sacredness of his temple were disregarded. In a flourish of irreverence, Belshazzar ordered that the holy vessels secured from God's temple during the conquest of Jerusalem be brought as wine cups for Babylon's feast.

Belshazzar was safe—he thought. But judgment would fall upon him that night. The Persians diverted the course of the Euphrates and penetrated Babylon's defenses by funneling troops under the city's walls through the drained riverbed. The city was conquered. Belshazzar was killed and Darius the Mede became king. The party was over. The prophet's words rang true and echo still:

"God cannot be mocked" (Gal. 6:7).

"The wrath of God is being revealed . . . against all the godlessness and wickedness of men" (Rom. 1:18).

"God will bring every deed into judgment, including every hidden thing, whether it is good or evil" (Eccles. 12:14).

Beware!

God says to every person, "Beware!" There is no man-made wall so high, no human fortress so secure, no activity so hidden that it can protect sinfulness from the wrath of God. We must consider that truth not only in the context of this ancient account of an arrogant king, but in terms of our lives today. There are walls we, too, try to erect to hide our sin from the eyes of God. But we must see the walls for what they are—foolish defenses that must be abandoned for our own ultimate welfare.

Human Security Won't Last

Belshazzar was hardly the first (nor the last) to believe that his sin was protected by a wall of human achievement. When *Forbes* magazine last figured the salary of stockbroker Ivan Boesky, the investment expert was making more that $100 million a year. Surely this was a secure man! But then the Securities and Exchange Commission discovered Boesky's illegal insider stock trading, and the King of Wall Street was ruined. *Mene, Tekel, Peres,* whispers God's Word.

Even more secure, in human terms, was Ferdinand Marcos of the Philippines. As absolute dictator of his isolated nation, he had his own personal army. In addition, because his country hosted U.S. naval and air bases, he also had the protection of the most powerful nation in the world. The Marcos domination was so complete and so corrupt that he bilked billions of dollars from his impoverished nation. Murder, theft, and political manipulation were such powerful tools of intimidation that it seemed no one could challenge him. From any reasonable human perspective, Marcos's security was beyond assault. But the island president was eventually numbered out, weighed, and found wanting, divided and ruined. His nation rallied behind the Christian wife of a slain political rival. She had no political experience or military training, but Corazon Aquino defeated Marcos, the Filipino Belshazzar. The Scriptures echo through the headlines: *Mene, Tekel, Peres.*

Although stories that make the headlines are impressive, they may not challenge us personally. The fame, power, and wealth of such notorious figures remove them from our reality. They are so unlike us that their stories seem to be interesting caricatures from distant morality plays. Until we see the impact of God's judgment in lives that seem "real," we may be remotely interested but unchanged. So consider the account of another man, someone more like us—a man whose life demonstrates the reality of a living God.

He was a frugal man. Beginning as a driver for a road-construction company, he saved every spare penny he earned. Before he was twenty-five he had saved enough to buy his own dump truck and become his own boss. He kept on saving. He bought another dump truck and then another. By the time he was thirty, he owned a truck line. His business went so well that he eventually bought the company that had first hired him as a driver. With a virtual monopoly on road-construction contracting and trucking services in his rural Tennessee community, this man became wealthy beyond his dreams.

He was a Christian man. As his business prospered, the local church leaders recognized the potential advantages of his involvement, so they asked him to become an officer in the church. They asked repeatedly, but he always turned them down. He was busy doing other things. These "other things" more and more began to dominate his life.

He was a man under pressure. Reports began to circulate in town about shady business deals and improperly handled contracts. His personality became more intense. His anger boiled more quickly. He began to drink more. The tension between the man and his wife became common gossip. The oldest son fled the family pressures by getting married in an ill-considered relationship. Two younger daughters rebelled, turned to drugs, and tuned out responsibility altogether.

He was a man in trouble. The business still occupied him. But there were new pressures there, too. The rapid expansion of the company caused cash-flow problems. Banks, listening to more rumors about mismanagement and misappropriation, became reticent to loan him money. Although the man finally turned to the church, it was not spiritual help he wanted. He asked old friends in the church to trust him and invest in his business because it was "totally secure." Many believed him, and some invested their life's savings in the firm.

He became a man in ruin. For reasons that are still not clear, the youngest daughter one day "borrowed" a neighbor's car. Joy-riding down a rain-slickened country road, she crossed the center line and plowed head-on into oncoming traffic. She lay in intensive care for thirteen months before she began recovering. The hospital costs were astronomical. The court battles between insurance companies and with passengers injured in the other vehicles still continue, years later. But, while the litigation awaits settlement, no one pays the bills except the family. In the first year after the accident, the family was charged $750,000 in medical bills. They lost the construction business and the investments of their church friends. In the second year they lost the truck line. In the third year they filed for bankruptcy. Today the once-wealthy businessman pumps gas at a service station in his hometown under the scorn of former investors and the ridicule of former friends.

The trek from truck driver to millionaire took about forty

years. The plunge from wealthy businessman to service station attendant took about four. The accident that caused the empire to fall took about three seconds: *Mene, Tekel, Peres.*

There is no human wall so high that it can protect us from the judgment of God. No matter how great the man, how hidden the means, or how long the practice has continued, God will ultimately prevail. His Word is true, and his justice is sure. In the Bible, in the newspaper, in the lives of the people we know, God warns us to beware of his holy judgment. Human security is an illusion that can vanish in a flash and will never endure beyond God's judgment.

Spiritual Insulation Won't Work

Since God speaks so plainly to warn us of the consequences of sin, why do so many continue to ignore him? One reason, of course, is that many do not believe in a living and just God. But there must be other reasons. Daniel reminded King Belshazzar that through his predecessor, Nebuchadnezzar, he knew all about God's judgment. Still the new king did not humble himself (5:22). Why do so many of us continue in sin although we *do* believe in a living God and realize that no human accomplishment secures us against his wrath? One reason is that Christians often believe that "putting on Christ" (see Gal. 3:27) provides spiritual insulation against God's righteous judgment in this life. Nothing could be further from the truth or a greater offense to God.

Belshazzar praised the gods of silver, gold, bronze, iron and wood—*the gods of his own making* (5:23). He continued in sin because he trusted these gods to protect him. So, too, do some believers continue in sin because of a god whose attributes they invent to protect them. Since they affirm that Jesus died for their sins and that God forgives whatever they confess, they believe they can do as they please. "Sure," they reason, "God doesn't want us to be 'really bad'—but ordinary business lies, ungodly entertainments, academic compromises, residual anger toward a brother, neglect of church work—these things don't really count. After all, God knows we're just human." Such shallow Christians wrap themselves in some pious half-truths about "everyone's tendency to sin" and so believe they are insulated from sin's real consequences. They fool only themselves. The god that they imagine will protect them is not the God of Daniel or of any other true child of God.

Notice at what moment in Belshazzar's feast God inscribed his judgment. The writing appeared when the king used the vessels from the temple to drink his wine and praise his gods. God revealed his wrath at precisely the moment when what was intended to be kept holy was used for sin. Fellow Christian, the Bible says that *you* now serve as God's vessel, his "jar of clay" (2 Cor. 4:7). God intends for your life and testimony to be holy. If you begin filling with sin and using for unholy purposes the vessel God has made sacred with the blood of his own Son, do not imagine you have any security against his wrath.

No Scripture says God will deal less harshly with your unrepented sin because you are a believer. The Bible says that to whom much is given, much is required (Luke 12:48). Israel was given the promise of the covenant, but for her sins she languished in Babylonian captivity. To us has been given the fulfillment of covenant promises in the sacrificial provision of God's own Son, who died for our sins. Surely it is foolish to think that we could dip our hands in the shed blood of Jesus and with impunity smear it over continuing greed, lust, and anger. Surely we cannot realistically imagine we could collect Christ's blood to use as a cover for personal advantage, evil excuse, and deliberate sin without expecting the righteous anger of his Holy Father. If we really knew the God of Daniel, we could not so abuse his Son. It is the worst abuse of faith to try to use the blood poured from Christ's wounds as spiritual insulation from divine wrath so that we can continue in sin. Yet how often do we (with the cross before our eyes) clothe ourselves self-righteously in the exemption from judgment we *mistakenly* believe is our "reward" for accepting Jesus as our Lord and Savior! There is no spiritual insulation that will hide sin from the piercing eye of God the Father. Likewise, the knowledge of biblical truth is no protection against God's judgment.

Spiritual knowledge cannot insulate anyone from the consequences of sin, as recent events have shown. Infrequent as such backsliding may be, the stories of Jim and Tammy Bakker, Jimmy Swaggart, and other popular media figures are instructive and well known. Such prideful tales of power, payoffs, and adultery are more sad than spicy. The parties themselves now admit that, somewhere in their vast material and ministerial successes, priorities became confused. In the ruin of reputations and ministry that has followed the scandals, the Word of God speaks without confusion: *Mene, Tekel, Peres.*

But these news accounts are again of persons whose extravagancies and well-publicized ministries may make God's message seem remote. It may be painful to bring the truth closer to home, but Daniel's warning must not go unheeded. Only weeks before I began writing this chapter, the head of one of this nation's largest campus ministries held a news conference to announce his resignation. He explained that while speaking at conferences, conducting seminars, and writing books on organizing one's spiritual life, he had also been committing adultery. So fell this man, one of the most gifted preachers of our day, a biblically solid and spiritually sensitive minister. Even as he resigned he could not ignore the Word of God. Among his stated reasons for resigning was setback after setback he had seen in his ministry over the two preceding years. He believed God was judging his hidden sin, and he could no longer bear to see others damaged by his transgressions. Some of my friends who knew this minister better than I were stunned by the news. They wept in unbelief and grief. They wept in doubt about themselves if one apparently so strong could be so weak. I weep with them. God weeps, too: *Mene, Tekel, Peres.*

If headlines are not enough, the judgment of those we love—those most like us—screams that we must heed God's warnings. In one way I have come to dread going to the national assemblies of evangelicals. It seems almost a certainty that I will hear of someone else I know who has been forced from the ministry. This year I learned of two more friends whose immorality killed their ministries. The fact that they are my friends is even more devastating, for I realize these are men like me. I am no better: I cannot pretend their error is due to some personality flaw I do not share. I am scared by their sins. I should be. If I do not appropriately fear their consequences, I may not adequately avoid their sins. I must always be afraid I do not fear sin enough.

I fear already we may no longer be as horrified by such unrighteousness as we should be. Both times I was told of my friends' sin and of the loss of their ministries the same phrase was used. I was told they left the ministry "for the usual reason." God help us if the evangelical church, which stands for the enduring truth of the Word of God, now regards adultery as "the usual reason" pastors leave ministries. We have not feared sin enough if adultery is becoming so common among our leaders that it can be considered the most frequent factor in a minister's downfall. God says, ". . . your sin will find you out" (Num. 32:23); "For God will bring every deed into judgment, including every hidden thing . . ." (Eccles. 12:14).

Mene, Tekel, Peres. Even though Belshazzar did not know the meaning of these words, his knees knocked, and his face turned pale when they appeared on the wall. How much more should a holy fear of sin seize believers, who know what the words meant for him and still mean for us? God says to all of us through Daniel, "Beware!"

Grieve

Daniel's message includes more than a warning about sin's consequences. There is weeping, too. It may be difficult to perceive Daniel's grief until one remembers the narratives that precede this passage and notices the language that permeates it. Four times in chapter five, the biblical writer reminds us that Nebuchadnezzar was the "father" of Belshazzar's rule. While the term signifies "predecessor" more than actual parent, its repeated reference implies something even more profound. For more than forty years Daniel nurtured, loved, and ultimately changed the life of Babylon's mightiest king. Now, only a generation later, the impact of so great a transformation seems lost. Belshazzar was as corrupt as his "father" ever was! How Daniel's heart must have grieved, as he focuses attention on the spiritual victory in Nebuchadnezzar's life in contrast to Belshazzar's subsequent surrender to wickedness (5:21, cf. vv. 22–24).

The grief the prophet must have felt over the king's sin is even more evident when the purpose of Daniel's book is considered. Daniel wrote as God's spokesman and instructor for all times. God is reminding us that sin can (and often does) re-infect a people. Israel was purified time after time, only to sink again into contamination. In fact, Israel was in bondage throughout Daniel's lifetime *because* of their repeated idolatry. God pointedly warned Israel with the object lesson of Belshazzar that sin resulted in judgment, but the warning was evidence of his desire that Israel not harm itself by continuing in evil. By indicating this great concern, God discloses how much grief he experiences when we sin. Our awareness of his grief for our hurt should further our love for him and strengthen our resistance to sin (see Eph. 4:30). Perhaps it is in part because we do not often share this sense of grief over others' sin and the inevitable consequences that the church seems so powerless against evil today.

Just as Daniel grieved over the judgment that surely would follow Nebuchadnezzar's sin (4:19), he lamented the decline of Babylon's commitment (5:22). Daniel's grief—which reflected God's grief—was recorded to turn God's people from sin but also to remind us that we are to feel sorrow when others sin. Are our friends and family members wandering far off course because they know no one will really care if they are lost or left behind? Most of us are quick to point out evil and even quicker to judge, glad we are not caught in such sin. But are we grieving for those whom sin has led astray? Are we so proud of our own blessings and "goodness" that we have lost the capacity to weep for those who have stumbled? There is much for which to grieve. And until we again see clearly and feel deeply the reasons to weep, we will have little influence with those who need the message of God's care. If we do not grieve for the sinner, we will have little power over the sin.

The consequences of our inability or refusal to grieve over the effects of sin may nowhere be more evident than in the church's handling of the sexual conduct of today's young people. Why do our teens not listen when the church says, "Tsk, tsk," to promiscuity? We tell them that premarital intercourse is unbiblical, but the ineffectiveness of our words is staggering. Nearly 75 percent of young men and 50 percent of young women in this country are sexually active before marriage. And Christian youth leaders like Josh McDowell say the figures are not significantly different for young people in evangelical churches. Why has the church lost power over the sin that is so rampant among its most precious members, its children? The temptation always is to blame others. The church blames parents for their leniency, especially for not monitoring their children's entertainments. Parents blame the church for not providing better youth programs. Parents and church blame a culture that inundates the young with sexually suggestive music, fashions, commercials, and movies. We have been blaming all sorts of things a long time. It has not done much good. Blaming is easier than grieving, but it seems to have little effect on sin.

Until the church learns to express grief for sinners as eloquently as it vents rage at their sin, the devastation of the young will continue. We must grieve for children having children, for children having abortions, for children so desperate for affection that they do not even know when they are being used or are using others. We know statistically that when sex enters a teenage relationship, a very bitter and quick end to that relationship usually follows. As suicide climbs to rank second as the leading cause of death among teens, psychologists tell us we are seeing evidence of just how bitter the end to a teen relationship can be when it included sex. Our young people are so lonely, so scared of homosexuality, so geared to peer values that they naively seek to cement relationships with the very adhesive that endangers their lives as well as their love. Are we grieving enough?

Do we grieve for the guilt taken into marriage? Do we weep for the damage to intimacy when the oneness God intended for a man and wife is eroded by painful memories, secret fears, and inevitable comparisons. Statisticians tell us the incidence of divorce is higher among those sexually active before marriage. The scars of teenage sex can take a lifetime to fade. It is time to weep. As a church, or as parents, we may be embarrassed, angered, or chagrined by our children's sexual behavior. But until we are grief-stricken, we have only demonstrated our ignorance, intolerance, and lack of compassion. If we loved as much as we blame—if we cared as much as we chide—our weeping for the wounds our young inflict on themselves just might penetrate the siren song of sexual romance that lures them to hurts beyond their estimation.

When Jesus looked over the people of Jerusalem, so immersed in sin and so hardened to his message that they soon would murder him, *he wept.* Jesus knew how to express rage and umbrage, but his first response to the devastation of sin was grief: "O Jerusalem, Jerusalem . . . how often I have longed to gather your children together, as a hen gathers her chicks under her wings, but you were not willing." Grief for sinners drove Jesus to the cross where sin was overpowered. If we are to have power over sin today, grief must drive us to our knees. It is easy to be angry with sin, easy to blame. But grieving for sin is hard work, calling for the deepest searching of our own hearts. We must shed these tears as though they were a rare, life-giving potion that alone could save a dying child. Without grief we are powerless over the sin that threatens us all.

In my own ministry I have seen how powerless is anger at sin if it is not accompanied by grief for sinners. I have learned, through what now brings me shame, that judgment without tears damages the Gospel. As a pastor, I watched over a period of years as a young woman in our church grew in the Lord. I will call her Debbie. A young teen, she came to us soon after her abusive and alcoholic father had abandoned the family. She had almost no Christian background, but through Sunday school and church camp experiences Debbie eventually committed her life to the Lord and blossomed in Him. She became a leader in our youth group and a wonderful testimony to other young people. She often took special care to befriend young people who also had troubled family backgrounds. Debbie shared her own life and the Lord's love.

When she graduated from high school, however, Debbie confronted the harsh realities facing many young women in poor, small towns. Without the means or desire for college, and without good job opportunities, she decided to get married. Sadly, her choice reflected the only family relationships she had known. The young man to whom she became engaged already had an alcohol problem, had bounced from one dead-end job to another, was currently unemployed—and, worst, was not a Christian. When I heard that a wedding was likely, I went to Debbie and expressed concern. She acknowledged that her "friend" was not a believer, said she remembered the Bible's instructions that believers should marry "only in the Lord," and promised to obey God's Word in her choice of whom she would marry. Three months later she came asking me to marry her to the very same young man. I was miffed. Debbie seemed to be ignoring everything I had said and everything she had promised.

Debbie assured me her fiance had become a Christian and

we set a time to talk about his faith and their plans. The conversation at our meeting made it very evident the young man did not have the slightest idea of what a Christian was and, furthermore was not the least interested. Now my anger began to boil. Debbie later confessed to friends she had decided to coach the young man on what to say to trick me into marrying them. Debbie was deliberately defying the Scriptures, had broken her word to me, and was now actively trying to deceive me. The whole situation made me furious. I called Debbie into my office, rebuked her for lying to me, and said I could not in good conscience marry the two unless both agreed genuinely to commit themselves to the Lord. Their response was to go to a church down the street to be married. That pastor did not know them and did not ask questions.

It was not until months later that I saw my sin. It was not that my decision was unbiblical; Scripture clearly forbids the wedding of believers and unbelievers (Matt. 19:5; 1 Cor. 7:39; 2 Cor. 6:14–7:2). My attitude was wrong and, therefore, made me increasingly helpless in dealing with Debbie. I became angry, but I did not grieve. Here was a young woman who had known alcoholism and abuse all her life. She knew no other family world. When she had the opportunity to make a new family world, she chose to marry back into her nightmare. She did not even have the perspective to know she was in a nightmare. And yet I did not grieve. So blinded was I by rage and vain concern for my own position, I lost sight of Debbie's pain. Is the reason she did not listen—could not listen—because she saw I did not care enough about her to grieve? Anger is no substitute for tears. Without weeping, the walls of sin are impenetrable however righteous our indignation may be.

Among the saddest words of Scripture are those echoed three times in the first chapter of Romans: "God gave them over to the sinful desires of their hearts." Paul's words remind us that sin is so terrible in itself that the worst punishment may simply be to let it rule the day. God may simply let people have their way when they persist in sin. The tragic results are worth grieving over. I have pastored long enough to know just what it may mean for sin to run its course. I have seen the troubled marriages that result when believers marry unbelievers, thus ignoring the directives of Scripture (see 2 Cor. 6:14–18). I have tried to comfort believing wives when tears of pain stream down their faces over children who are following the paths of unbelieving husbands. I have watched in helplessness as an already shallow faith becomes a sham when Christian marries non-Christian.

When God's people disobeyed, the Old Testament prophet Ezekiel cried out in pain because he saw the Lord's glory leave their temple. When God's people disobey him today, the experience of his blessing departs their lives. Until we weep over the tragedy of sin, we will not pray, work, and love as we should, for we will not have grieved as we ought. It is not enough that our knees quake in *fear* of sin's consequences. Our knees must give way in *grief* over the sinner, else we are powerless to confront or correct the sin.

Repent

Where is the grace in all of this? Are fear and grief all Daniel can offer from God in this chapter? No. The mercy of the previous chapters has not vanished. In fact, God's very warnings are proof of God's love. If he did not care, he would not warn.

As a child I loved the evenings when the kids in our family would sit by my father's chair while he read us stories aloud. One of our favorites was the poem "The Highwayman." The poem tells of an adventurer who robs the coaches of English aristocrats. The daring highwayman is in love with an innkeeper's daughter and courts her by night, when the coast is clear. The authorities learn of the romance, and one twilight before the highwayman arrives, British soldiers invade the inn. They tie the innkeeper's daughter at the window so her lover will see her and believe the way is safe. Then, lest she try to warn him in any way, the soldiers gag the maiden and tie at her heart a musket that will fire at the slightest movement.

Unaware of the soldiers that wait to cut him down, the highwayman gallops ever closer to his destruction. He sees his love at the window. She hears his horse's hoofs on the lane. The soldiers cock their muskets. Nearer to the arms he loves, nearer to his destruction, the highwayman comes riding. Then, just as he is about to enter musket range, a premature shot rings out, warning him to turn back. The highwayman reins in his horse and turns as the frustrated soldiers shoot a futile volley. Only one shot found its mark. That one true shot was from the musket that fired the warning, the musket aimed at the heart of the innkeeper's daughter. She had warned at the expense of her life, so great was her love.

Daniel's warnings also express a great love, though they are only the early strains of a clarion call echoing through history and culminating at Calvary. There at the cross our Lord demonstrated how great is his love by sacrificing his life to warn us of the destruction that awaits us if we do not turn from sin. This was not the first warning God had sounded, only the most poignant. Through Daniel's accounts of Nebuchadnezzar and Belshazzar, God had previously warned that repentance leads to blessing and rebellion to destruction. God warned in the writing on the wall that we all live in a just universe where sin will be punished. The message of the cross completes that warning. The hymnist Thomas Kelly points to the cross on which the Son of God died and writes:

> You who think of sin but lightly
>   Nor suppose the evil great
> Here may view its nature rightly,
>   Here its guilt may estimate.

The cross stands both as God's ultimate warning of the consequences of sin, and as the greatest expression of his love for sinners. If God did not love so completely, he would not so graciously warn. The cross is the death cry of a Savior, warning those he loves to turn from what will do them infinite harm.

Mene, Tekel, Peres is not handwriting meant just for Belshazzar. It is God's message to us all. By his hand God warns us of our sin. On the cross of Jesus we see that handwriting in its boldest and brightest strokes, for there the script is written in the blood of God's own Son. But the real glory of that blood is that it does more than warn. It saves. The blood that spells out our sin so vividly is the same blood that blots out the handwriting of our condemnation. The blood of Jesus beacons and beckons. It beacons a warning to all who will look, testifying that God judges sin. "Turn back," the blood warns, "turn back from the sin that leads to your hurt and this destruction." At the same time the blood beckons. It summons sinners to be covered and cleansed by the crimson flow that God lovingly provides for all who truly repent. "Come," cries the blood, "come away from your guilt and enter the forgiving, comforting, strengthening presence of the Savior." The blood beckons all to bend the knee before the Savior in humble confession to claim his full salvation. God warns us of his judgment so that we will seek the Son who has already assumed it.

Growing in Grace

Sin is pleasant only for a season; it has a limited appeal. Since God knows this better than any of us, he warns us as clearly as possible about sin—its consequences and his judgment. The warnings may seem harsh, but their intent is clear. God only wants us to turn from the sin that will hurt us and return to the arms that will hold us in safety. As a human father lovingly reserves his sternest warnings for the greatest dangers his child will face, our heavenly Father carefully measures his terms to warn us of the eternal dangers to our growth in grace.

Over the past two years I probably have added to my reputation as an academic eccentric by wandering the woods of our seminary campus to collect tree seedlings. I have been transplanting a great many young trees into our yard to create a barrier between our house and the nearby highway. A few weeks ago I found a suitable seedling deep in the woods and began to dig it up. As I began to pry the small tree from the ground, topsoil fell off the upper roots, and I discovered a most unusual growth pattern. The seedling was growing up through the loop of a discarded pull tab from a soda can. You know what would have happened if I had not pulled the seedling up and discovered the metal tab. The tree would have been okay for a while. Inevitably, though, the direction in which the plant was growing would cause its destruction. Temporarily, what seemed like a convenient and acceptable course would merely keep the tree from maturing and reaching its potential. Finally—and no one knows at what day or hour it would happen—the tab would strangle the tree.

Still, I wanted that pitiful little tree: I had a purpose for it. And so I began to remove the threatening tab from the seedling. I threaded the metal loop over the tender branches and young leaves. In the process I bruised some of the small limbs and tore some of the leaves, but the process was necessary to save the tree. It was a harsh mercy!

Later I realized that God's mercy sometimes must be just as severe. We, too, may have sin hidden from the view of others. Its dangers may even be hidden from our own awareness. But nothing is hidden from God. He sees every sin that threatens to strangle a healthy faith and cripple our growth in grace. Still, he has a purpose for our lives and loves us too much to let that sin overcome us. So he extricates us from our danger by warning us of the peril we are in and showing us the way to thrive in him. Being freed from our sin is not always painless. Sometimes we must be bruised and torn before we are truly free to grow. Sometimes God's mercy seems harsh. But God acts in love, and he only desires that we grow in his grace.

Although the message of God's judgment is never pleasant, we must listen carefully. However dark or hidden away our sin, however secure we think we are, we must listen. God is saying, "Your sin will surely find you out, for I bring every deed into judgment including every hidden thing. You must turn from it, my child. Go back from the sin that will destroy what is most precious to you and to me. I judge sin. I desire to show mercy. I love you and gave my Son for you. Come back to the arms that will embrace you with love and life. Come back, my child, come back."

Mene, Tekel, Peres.

6

The Sound of a Broom

(Daniel 6)

The Word

Sunday-school pictures of a ruddy-faced lad in a lions' den have scant resemblance to the actual situation described in this last significant episode in Daniel's life story. Daniel was more than ninety years old when these events unfolded. You might think he had earned a little rest and relaxation for those "retirement years," but God was still using the faithful prophet. Age alone is never a barrier to spiritual usefulness.

A new king reigned over Babylon. Darius the Mede was the conquering ruler who, like the Babylonian kings before him, recognized Daniel's wisdom. When Darius selected the aging prophet for his cabinet, Daniel became one of only three administrators who governed Babylon. But Daniel's rise to power was still incomplete. Daniel so excelled at his post that the king decided to put him solely in charge of the whole Babylonian government.

Other cabinet members and lesser officials were not pleased. They tried to dig up some dirt to ruin Daniel. But he was too honest. No trumped-up charge would stick. Then the growing jealousy of the evil officials mutated into a warped ingenuity. "Let's use Daniel's religious convictions to trap him," they plotted.

The officials appealed to the pagan king's pride. "O king," they said, "you are so great no one should pray to anyone but you. It is actually an insult for anyone to recognize any being greater than your magnificence. Why not issue a royal decree, which cannot be challenged or altered, which will punish anyone who would insult your greatness by praying to anyone but you?"

The king's pride trapped him. He ordered the lions' den for those who would pray to any god but him. Little did the king know of the fate his pride had determined for his trusted friend Daniel. The decree was issued and the lions' appetite whetted. Daniel now faced his greatest trial yet:

> [1]It pleased Darius to appoint 120 satraps to rule throughout the kingdom, [2]with three administrators over them, one of whom was Daniel. The satraps were made accountable to them so that the king might not suffer loss. [3]Now Daniel so distinguished himself among the administrators and the satraps by his exceptional qualities that the king planned to set him over the whole kingdom. [4]At this, the administrators and the satraps tried to find grounds for charges against Daniel in his conduct of government affairs, but they were unable to do so. They could find no corruption in him, because he was trustworthy and neither corrupt nor negligent. [5]Finally these men said, "We will never find any basis for charges against this man Daniel unless it has something to do with the law of his God."
>
> [6]So the administrators and the satraps went as a group to the king and said: "O King Darius, live forever! [7]The royal administrators, prefects, satraps, advisers and governors have all agreed that the king should issue an edict and enforce the decree that anyone who prays to any god or man during the next thirty days, except to you, O king, shall be thrown into the lions' den. [8]Now, O king, issue the decree and put it in writing so that it cannot be altered—in accordance with the laws of the Medes and Persians, which cannot be repealed." [9]So King Darius put the decree in writing.
>
> [10]***Now when Daniel learned that the decree had been published, he went home to his upstairs room where the windows opened toward Jerusalem. Three times a day he got down on his knees and prayed, giving thanks to God, just as he had done before.*** [11]Then these men went as

a group and found Daniel praying and asking God for help.
[12]So they went to the king and spoke to him about his royal
decree: "Did you not publish a decree that during the next
thirty days anyone who prays to any god or man except to
you, O king, would be thrown into the lions' den?"

The king answered, "The decree stands—in accordance
with the laws of the Medes and Persians, which cannot be
repealed."

[13]Then they said to the king, "Daniel, who is one of the
exiles from Judah, pays no attention to you, O king, or to the
decree you put in writing. He still prays three times a day."
[14]When the king heard this, he was greatly distressed; he was
determined to rescue Daniel and made every effort until sun-
down to save him.

[15]Then the men went as a group to the king and said to
him, "Remember, O king, that according to the law of the
Medes and Persians no decree or edict that the king issues
can be changed."

[16]So the king gave the order, and they brought Daniel and
threw him into the lions' den. The king said to Daniel, "May
your God, whom you serve continually, rescue you!"

[17]A stone was brought and placed over the mouth of the
den, and the king sealed it with his own signet ring and with
the rings of his nobles, so that Daniel's situation might not
be changed. [18]Then the king returned to his palace and spent
the night without eating and without any entertainment
being brought to him. And he could not sleep.

***[19]At the first light of dawn, the king got up and hurried
to the lions' den. [20]When he came near the den, he called
to Daniel in an anguished voice, "Daniel, servant of the
living God, has your God, whom you serve continually,
been able to rescue you from the lions?"***

***[21]Daniel answered, "O king, live forever! [22]My God sent
his angel, and he shut the mouths of the lions. They have
not hurt me, because I was found innocent in his sight.
Nor have I ever done any wrong before you, O king."***

[23]The king was overjoyed and gave orders to lift Daniel out
of the den. And when Daniel was lifted from the den, no
wound was found on him, because he had trusted in his God.

[24]At the king's command, the men who had falsely accused

Daniel were brought in and thrown into the lions' den, along with their wives and children. And before they reached the floor of the den, the lions overpowered them and crushed all their bones.

25Then King Darius wrote to all the peoples, nations and men of every language throughout the land:

"May you prosper greatly!

26"I issue a decree that in every part of my kingdom people must fear and reverence the God of Daniel.

"For he is the living God and he endures forever; his kingdom will not be destroyed, his dominion will never end.

27He rescues and he saves; he performs signs and wonders in the heavens and on the earth. He has rescued Daniel from the power of the lions."

28So Daniel prospered during the reign of Darius and the reign of Cyrus the Persian.

Daniel 6 (*Emphasis added*)

"Whisk-Whisk"

Four more days and the young girl would be seventeen. It would be her father's birthday, too, but this year there would be no party. America was mired in the Great Depression, and Dad lay dying. Instead of gathering presents, the family gathered around a rickety bed and prayed over the sound of his labored breathing until it was silenced forever.

On the day of the funeral, the widow and her seven children trudged through the mud with a small crowd to a simple grave. Mainly women friends came, because the men could not afford to miss work. The teenage girl had to borrow a dress for the occasion. When the family went home, she carefully folded it smooth and lay next to it on her bed.

A sense of desolation seemed to crush her. It was over—not just the funeral—everything. Seven kids, no real income, the house so heavily mortgaged it would not be theirs for long. She was old enough to know these things, and to despair because of them. Even the silence of the room seemed to weigh on her and press hope out of her.

And then she heard it. Breaking the oppressive silence came the tentative *Whisk-Whisk* of a broom on the kitchen floor. Then the sound came again, more determined this time. *Whisk-Whisk.* Her mother, who had not spoken for three days, was back about her duties—the broom went *whisk-whisk.* The girl would write later in her diary how powerful was the gentle sound of her mother's resumption of that simple household task. It kindled new hope and faith in the child's heart since it seemed to be saying, "The world is not entirely fallen in, all is not lost. There is hope, and life will go on." This message was heard in the sound of a broom, which indicated there were still things worth doing. Her mother was pressing on. The assumption of the everyday duty expressed her faith that things would work out—that there was still a future. Faith brought forth the duty, even as the duty expressed the faith. In the gentle rhythm of the broom came a song of hope and eventual triumph as faith and duty joined hands for the immediate task. *Whisk-Whisk* went the broom, and each repeated stroke whispered, "Faith and duty, faith and duty."

It was enough to convince the girl to rise from the bed, ready to take up her own tasks and resume her life with new courage and hope. Many difficulties lay ahead. Tragedy still cast its shadow. But life was no longer empty, hopeless, and purposeless. All the "What-shall-we-do?" and "What-comes-next?" questions were being answered in part by the sound of a broom that sang, "Faith and duty, faith and duty."

As any book concludes, there is the temptation for its author to end with a boom. But I prefer to end with the softer sound of a broom. The above adaptation of an Elisabeth Elliot account seems to capture the truths of the final stage of Daniel's life. The attitude and actions that always led the prophet from trial to triumph echo in the broom's *Whisk-Whisk.* "Faith and duty," those whisks say—words which lead us from difficulty to victory in our Christian lives today. Against the adversity and temptations that threaten to crush us comes the calming echo of a prophet's "broom." He sweeps away the confusion of our circumstances and the complexity of our questions with a gentle reminder: a call to faith and duty.

We cry out in our anguish, "O God, tell me what to do. What do you expect of me?" Through his prophet God replies that faith is the remedy for our doubts and frailty, and duty the answer to difficulty. No matter the magnitude of the trial or the seeming senselessness of God's requirements, where there is faith and duty there is holy triumph ahead.

The Duty of Faith

The duty God expects of his people is evident in Daniel's faithful prayer. In response to a royal decree forbidding prayer upon pain of horrible death, Daniel does as he had always done. ". . . Three times a day he got down on his knees and prayed, giving thanks to his God, just as he had done before" (6:10). Although duty seemed to promote disaster, Daniel remained faithful. He did not question whether praying was the wisest course of action or whether the probable consequences outweighed God's requirements. He simply did his duty.

Perhaps such a steadfast commitment strikes us as neither significant nor relevant today. After all, Daniel was a prophet—a supersaint. It was in character for him to be incredibly loyal. But stereotyping this man of faith with such a larger-than-life role actually ruins his testimony. By calling Daniel "unreal," and his commitment to duty "not the norm," we may rob ourselves of the help God intends to provide us through this prophet. Daniel does demonstrate *attainable faith;* he represents the accessibility of God's victory in our lives. Through his prophet, God shows us that faithfulness to holy duty in the midst of tragedy or temptation yields overpowering triumph.

Duty in the Face of Tragedy

God's victory over Daniel's foes at this stage in the prophet's life indicates how duty can be a powerfully effective tool for forging triumph out of personal tragedy. Bible teachers often refer to Daniel as one of the great "success stories" of the Scriptures, based on a very selective gathering of facts from the prophet's life. A more honest weighing of *all* the facts might cause us to speak less of "Daniel the Great" and more of "Daniel the Frustrated." Each of his victories apparently made but a fleeting spiritual impression on the people and culture around him. As far as Daniel knew, his life had been spent in fruitlessness and his impact on history was nil.

Daniel the Frustrated. Daniel had been ministering in this pagan land for most of a century. What did he have to show for it? Almost nothing. The people of Babylon were basically unchanged. Kingdoms had come and gone, but still the rulers were idolatrous, wicked, and cruel.

Still, all Daniel's trials might be considered worth the suffering and disappointment if there was some evidence that his ministry had borne fruit among his own people. Instead, not only was Babylon unchanged, but God's chosen people remained in captivity there despite Daniel's frequent promotions to positions of power. (And when these "chosen people" returned to Israel after Daniel's death, their spiritual understanding was so eroded they could not even remember God's words nor how they were supposed to worship him.) No revival swept through the captive nation as a result of Daniel's ministry. No national repentance resulted from his message. No one seemed to learn very much from Daniel!

Daniel himself seemed to have gained little, since his influence tended to come and go with purposeless frequency. He had offered a lifetime of honest administration and godly counsel in government service. Was he rewarded? No, for all his wisdom, integrity, and faithfulness, Daniel reaped the jealousy of peers, the hatred of the ungodly, a plot against his life, and a death sentence in a lions' den. And God expected more from him? Why? In the face of his apparent failures, what good was Daniel's duty?

The answer lies hidden in the last verse of this sixth chapter of Daniel. Because of his faithfulness to duty, "Daniel prospered during the reign of Darius and the reign of Cyrus the Persian." Daniel's influence outlasted Darius's reign. The prophet's duty was not completed until he touched the life of Cyrus the Persian, the ruler who would eventually return Israel to its homeland, setting the stage for the coming Messiah. Though Daniel did not live to see the full fruit of his labors, God used the faithful duty of this often-frustrated man to bring deliverance to a nation and prepare the world for salvation. All Daniel could see in his own life was failure, but God saw the opportunity for victory in his servant's unswerving devotion. Through the example of Daniel, we are reminded that God's triumphs are not to be measured by what human eyes can see but by faithfulness to duty.

Earl the Foundation. In a church I pastored there is an older man named Earl. He is one of those special men whom pastors come to identify as foundation stones of the churches they serve. Pastors come and go. Every church is shaken by its share of triumphs and tragedies, disputes and wrangles. But the foundation stones stand firm, and the church stands because of them. Earl is one of those foundation stones. He has simply been there, week in and week out, and year after year, for more than three-quarters of a century. When pastors have erred, when sheep have wandered, when wolves have crept in and scattered the flock or attacked him personally, Earl has remained faithful to his duty. Wherever his gifts have been needed, he has served gladly. When less mature parishioners have slandered his name out of jealousy for the respect he has earned, Earl has responded with silence and compassion. He has simply and faithfully done his duty.

Despite his great contributions to the life of the church, Earl's own life has contained much personal tragedy. He married late in life, though he would have been considered "quite a catch" in his youth. In those early days, Earl put aside his own interests and career to take care of the family farm and his ailing parents. Eventually, after his parents died of prolonged illnesses, Earl married and raised his family in the modest lifestyle provided by the small farm that had consumed his early career opportunities and much of his adult life.

Finally it seemed as though Earl's sacrifices might be rewarded. The local coal industry was booming, and his farm lay right over a huge vein of coal. A mining company began to work the vein on an adjacent property, and the value of Earl's land skyrocketed. When the company offered Earl a premium price for his entire farm, he sold his land and for the first time in his life tasted financial security. He bought a new home for himself and—since it was the nature of this man to sacrifice for others—he purchased homes for his children. There was still money left over, so (with an eye to the future) Earl wisely invested in home construction. He built homes of quality, characteristic of the man himself.

No one was prepared when the boom went bust! The most prudent investments soon looked very foolish. When changing federal pollution standards made the soft, high-sulphur coal of the region extremely difficult to market, many miners lost their jobs. The market for homes became nonexistent as families departed the region to search for work. Besides the mining decline, the rural economy experienced the double whammy of the national farm crisis. Family after family went bankrupt and moved away. There was no market for Earl's quality homes.

Earl went broke, losing not only the money invested in the new homes, but his own home and his children's homes. He never complained or spoke of his pain. Sunday after Sunday I watched the suffering man whom I loved and respected so highly. I learned to read what was behind Earl's firm handshake and jovial greeting. Somewhere deep in those eyes, always full of compassion for others, were hints of frustration and pain. Those eyes confessed, "I have failed!"

What did Earl do in the face of this great personal tragedy? He continued in his duty. He remained a foundation stone. When con men offered him quick but unethical ways out of his financial difficulties, he maintained his integrity. When the church was being racked by tensions created by the devastation of the local economy, Earl was steady and faithful in his support of the Lord's work. Surely temptations came to give in to bitterness, fear, and pessimism, but Earl never wavered from godliness. I believe we remained a church during those difficult years more because of Earl's commitment to duty than because of any pastoral effort of mine or financial plan or building program. He remained solidly in place—and we kept standing as a church.

To some, Earl's dutiful service may seem foolish and fruitless, especially in the light of his own personal difficulties. But I know there is nothing more dear to Earl's heart than the work of the Lord. He would have gladly given up all he lost—and more—if only one person would commit his life to Jesus Christ as a result. Of course, no one was saved as a direct result of Earl's losses, but because of his faithfulness our church survived the bad times. Earl became a beacon of hope and Christian maturity for the younger men in our congregation who were losing jobs and homes. With Earl's example and encouragement, they did not lose faith. Three of those young men are now in seminary, training to become pastors. And *this* young pastor now teaches at that seminary, in part because of supposed "successes" he experienced in that church (though this young paster knows who truly provided the stability to make the successes possible). The lives of all these young men in ministry will literally touch hundreds, perhaps thousands, and many will come to know Jesus as a result.

Earl may never see all the fruit of his labors, but the Lord triumphs through his duty nonetheless. Earl recognizes that his fondest dreams are being realized because God is using his duty for victory. This is more than enough reward for Earl. No personal tragedy can rob Earl of the joy of knowing that God is using him for wonderful spiritual purposes. Earl knows that God always triumphs in Christian duty.

We may not be able to see past our hurts and frustrations, so God tells us what the results will be. Where duty is observed, ultimate victory is assured as the tears of today are dried by the triumphs of tomorrow. Through the faithfulness of his people, God overcomes the dark forces of this world. Frustration and tragedy may come, but they cannot overwhelm God's purposes—or our usefulness when we continue in the duty he sets before us.

Duty in the Face of Temptation

Daniel's faithfulness to duty was challenged by more than personal tragedy. Surely we can identify with him in his struggle against the external evil about him! Consider how imposing were the forces with which he contended. He was alone in his stand of faith against all the other advisers of the king. The law—the unchangeable decree of the Medes and Persians—opposed Daniel, and even the king had no power to alter this law. Injustice ruled. Idolatry dominated. Daniel's people remained in powerless captivity. What could one man do against such overwhelming established evil? What would it matter if one person took a stand against an entire nation, culture, and tradition of godlessness? Who would even care if Daniel fulfilled his personal duty to God?

Do you recognize the temptation Daniel faced? It is the little voice that argues, "What *you* do will make no difference." It is the game children play with their parents, and adults play with God, when we want to get away with what we know is wrong. A young teenager asks his parents about going to see a movie with questionable sexual content. His mother replies, "No, John, you know we don't support that kind of entertainment." What is John likely to reply? "Aw, c'mon, Mom. They're not going to close down the theater just because I don't go." What is the implicit argument? "My little stand for godliness doesn't matter."

Adults use the same argument. We say to ourselves that this entertainment, this product, or this practice will go on whether or not we participate. Then we rationalize that—since what we do will make no difference—there is no duty required. Daniel teaches us that the call to duty remains even when sin seems unaffected by what we do. God requires our faithfulness though a sin may be so widespread that to oppose it places us in a position of ridicule and personal jeopardy. God says our duty is still to stand our ground.

Many sins have grown to levels of institutionalized acceptance in our culture. Their pervasiveness makes them difficult to resist, and their commonness makes them difficult even to see. Sensibilities grow dull to what inundates and surrounds. Our society's lust for violence is ingrained from our children's earliest years, even through their toys and entertainments. The national addiction to wealth and the images of material success prioritize the race for affluence over frugality, family, and faith. There is a general longing to flee daily pressures through drugs and other forms of escapism: sex, sports, parties, television, paramilitary games, the occult, and long meaningless weekends. Each of these evidences of a sin-sick culture is worth extended comment, but recent events in both the secular and religious sectors underscore the need to plead for Christian duty on two fronts. The institutionalized sins that have captured the media spotlight revolve around a crisis of integrity and a crisis of sexual license. Both indicate the erosion of traditional morality, even among believers. So overwhelming are these sins that it is no longer a foregone conclusion that Christians will see a reason for duty in these areas, much less do their duty.

1. *The Crisis of Integrity*

What do each of the following organizations or people have in common? Exxon, Drexel Burnham Lambert, General Dynamics, HUD, the NBA, E. F. Hutton, Southern Methodist University, Joseph Biden, the New York Stock Exchange, the

University of Illinois sports program, PTL, Ivan Boesky, the United States Air Force Academy, the United States Olympic Weight Lifting Team, Keith Hernandez, the Pentagon, the National Air Flight Controllers School, the United States Food and Drug Administration, Ashland Oil, the Chicago judicial system, the National Security Council, Hertz Corporation, John Tower, Jim Wright, the Central Intelligence Agency, IRS, the "Boz," Chrysler Corporation, Northwest Airlines, Dwight Gooden, NASA, the University of Oklahoma football program, the General Services Administration, the recent governors of at least five states, Anheuser-Busch Corporation, Lawrence Taylor, faith healers, the NFL, the United States Navy, Michael Deaver, General Motors, the Washington Post, Texaco. If you tire of reading this list, recognize that it could be much longer. As diverse as the individuals or organizations in the list may seem, they actually share something. Each person or institution cited has gained notoriety in the national news as either a party to scandal or a victim of its effects.

In every sphere of our culture—business, government, sports, education, religion—there is an integrity crisis. Long-accepted ethical codes of conduct have given way to the short-term pragmatics of ambition, profit, and pleasure. There have always been individuals willing to sell out their country, company, and/or responsibilities for personal gain, but the current pervasiveness of this attitude is amazing. We hardly blink at the latest headline scandals. If the Jim Bakker and Jimmy Swaggert stories had not been about men who were famous for decrying our society's ills, who would have lifted an eyebrow? Irony made the religious disgraces so interesting, not the novelty of their offenses. Scandal is unlikely to surprise us today.

The danger is that when a lack of integrity no longer shocks, it loses its reprehensibleness and gains acceptability. Listening to some businessmen, one gets the impression that the recent convictions of some corporate giants resulted more from a lack of savvy than a lack of ethics. Similarly, the improprieties of civil officials are denounced or defended on the basis of philosophical or political affiliations, not according to whether there has been a breach of the public trust.

The loss of an ethical consensus is evident at every level of our society, including the church. It is an obscenity that in the past ten years the number of federal officials under criminal indictment has increased from 50 to 500. But it is no less an obscenity than the disregard for law evident in the sale of radar "fuzz busters" and in ads for alterations to unleaded gasoline filler pipes at local muffler shops. Students shop for term papers in campus newspaper ads, and ministers buy sermons through pastoral journals and then preach them as originals. The pervasive acceptance of ethical compromises can be more dangerous than the actual compromises themselves. When we no longer recognize evil, we can no longer stop it.

Eyes that Cannot See. Three years ago I spoke at a church conference on the need for businessmen to commit themselves to integrity. I spoke candidly about my own experiences as a young adult working in a number of companies. In every case, within a few months of being employed, I was asked to participate in (or made aware of) business practices that were either unethical or illegal. For example, I told them about a supervisor who explained to me how to "fudge" on an expense account. "Use these techniques to give yourself a little bonus every now and then," he said. "Just don't give yourself any bigger bonuses than I give myself." I actually had co-workers enraged with me in the short time I worked there, since refusing to pad my own expense account made their expenses obviously exorbitant. As I detailed these and other experiences, along with some government statistics about white-collar crime, I urged the conference participants to guard their business practices with uncompromising integrity.

After my message, an expensively dressed businessman approached me and said he was offended by my comments.

"Businesses today have discovered that it simply is good business to operate ethically," he said. "We don't have any ethical problems in my company and, except for a few bad apples that make the headlines, I don't know of any companies that operate without complete integrity."

The articulate defense was made with enough volume and passion that it made quite an impression on me and attracted a small group of conferees. I was chagrined and embarrassed and began to wonder if my comments had been too strong. But, among the conferees that gathered around as the businessman gave me his assessment of my message, was that man's pastor. After the group had dispersed, the pastor took me aside. He said a number of people in his church worked for the same company as the businessman who had objected to my comments. "They have so many problems at that company," said the pastor, "that most of my people are being ripped apart by the ethical choices they are being forced to make. Please forgive the brother who objected. He's new in the faith and hasn't yet learned to see clearly."

The businessman had grown so accustomed to ethical erosion all around him that he was completely unaware of it. He was not lying when he said there were no unethical practices in his company. Since he really did not see the problems, he was powerless to do his duty in the face of these sins. I have since learned to gauge the spiritual maturity of people in many walks of life by their perceptiveness to the evils that surround them. If they are oblivious to the challenge of evil in their business or trade, it is rarely because of the absence of evil. More often their vision is not yet sufficiently refined by the Spirit of God. We are never in greater spiritual danger than when we are blind to evil.

The Watching World. How is the Christian to respond to the crisis of integrity in today's society? Ironically, one response might be joy! The best opportunity for even the smallest light of a Christian testimony to become a beacon is when the darkness is deepest. Duty shines brightly then.

Surrounded by deceit, corruption, and lies, Daniel's simple daily prayers made headlines in Babylon. Likewise, if integrity is a rare commodity in today's world, those who possess it will be known.

This message of the radiant power of duty amidst institutional darkness should encourage Christians. After all, how often do we fret over how we can be effective witnesses for Christ in the world? We memorize witnessing programs that we forget in two weeks (or hours?). We quake at the idea of door-to-door evangelism. When the pastor reminds us on Sunday of our duty to tell others about Jesus, we feel guilty but no more equipped and no less embarrassed to express our faith on Monday. Sometimes we get so frustrated over our inability to stand up for the Lord that we despair. We decide to leave witnessing to those more "gifted" and choose to live quiet lives of unobtrusive, inoffensive, and therefore *ineffective* Christianity. Daniel reminds us that it need not be so. By standing our ground, we stand up for Jesus.

Do you want to stand tall for the Lord? Do you want to have a vibrant and compelling testimony? Do not avoid the obvious. Do not sell yourself short. You have a powerful testimony, simply by doing your duty to God before a watching world. Christians who live honorable and honest lives to bring honor and glory to God are beacons for the gospel. Their witnessing is not in eloquent words, but in the careful application of God's Word to all of life. This testimony *wins* a hearing for the gospel, rather than *demands* that others listen.

In today's world it is obvious that those whose integrity is consistent, conscientious, and resistant to pressure will be noticed. Since such persons are apparently not the norm, they will stand out. And, by standing their ground, their commitment to and trust in Jesus is made known to the watching world.

Such devotion to duty is not easily maintained. In order to stand tall for God, Daniel sought help from the Lord on his knees. We must learn from Daniel's example. Holiness is not maintained by our resolve, but by the power of God at work in us (cf. Eph. 6:10). Duty to God requires dependence on him. While the crisis of integrity in our culture can fill us with eager anticipation of the opportunity for Christian witness, the accompanying threats to holiness must drive us to our knees to seek God's strength to stand for him.

Until we are humbled by the knowledge of our potential to yield to societal and professional pressures, we will not seek God with the total devotion required to serve him. We must confess our weakness to God and appeal for his strength, lest our "standing tall" be mere posturing. If a prophet like Daniel got down on his knees when duty called, how much more must we be willing to so humble ourselves? Especially when our devotion to duty appears to change nothing—and only jeopardizes our security—we need God's strength and support to persevere.

2. The Crisis of Sexual License

Sensitivity to our potential for weakness when faced with matters of integrity prepares us to consider another general threat to Christian duty. There is no plainer example of modern-day evil that threatens to surround and overwhelm us all than the sin of sexual license. Again, the temptation is to believe the sin is so widespread that it is senseless to resist (much less try to change things). But the effects of sexual license are so devastating that Christians must awaken to their duty and then resist with all the might God supplies.

The Flood. One day, as I completed my graduate studies at a state university, I took my books to a desk near an open library window to enjoy the sun and summer breezes while studying. The window overlooked the university quadrangle, and I soon noticed that some students below were also taking advantage of the warm weather. I could not help noticing—mainly because of what they were *not* wearing.

I was at that moment struck by the absurd choices we

believers sometimes make. We immerse our teens in the university culture of sexually suggestive (or explicit) music, movies, and books; move them many miles from family influence, Christian peers, and church leadership, and place them among people of different values in educational institutions where sexual immorality is the order of the day. But somehow we expect our youth to remain sexually pure although they are in danger of drowning in a flood of temptation!

Many respond, "Young adults have to become responsible for their actions and grow up sometime." Agreed. But *when* in their entire lives (even as mature believers) will most people be submitted to such persistent sexual pressures while so distant for so long from family and church influences? The church too often allows its children to grow up in a lions' den, without realizing they are in great danger of being eaten alive. I am not suggesting that Christian parents keep their children from college. I am willing to argue, however, for Christian young people and their parents to take as much care in sizing up the spiritual resources of a campus as they do in determining the quality of its business or engineering program. Is there a viable campus ministry? Are there sound, biblical churches in the area supporting Christian students? The dangers and temptations of life-scarring sin are simply too great to make decisions without regard for spiritual concerns.

A Harris Poll published in 1987 found that almost 60 percent of the nation's seventeen-year-olds were sexually experienced. Even sadder is the fact that the figures do not vary significantly in the Christian community. In his devastating survey of evangelical teens, published in 1988, Josh McDowell reported that almost 45 percent of the "churched youth" had sex by age eighteen. Josh McDowell is not speaking as a critic of the evangelical church. In fact, he has effectively ministered for years to young people in our nation's churches and colleges. His report sounds a warning that we simply cannot ignore the influences threatening our youth.

So pervasive is sexual license that even Christian leaders have grown calloused to the sin and its dangers. I was invited recently to a church officer's home for dinner. Because the meal was not quite ready, we went to the backyard, where the family's adolescent boys had set up a basketball hoop. After only a few minutes of a one-on-one game, we went into the boys' nearby clubhouse to find some chairs in which to collapse. Posters of *Playboy* pictures covered the clubhouse walls. At that point I expected my host to melt through the floor in embarrassment over his sons' "decorations." Instead, he explained that he knew all about the pinups. He said he allowed the pictures because he wanted his sons to get sexual exploration "out of their systems" while they were at home, before getting out into the "real world."

Understand, my host was no ordinary pew-warmer. He was a church leader, an ordained elder. According to the Bible, that meant he was supposed to be spiritually discerning (Rom. 12:2; Heb. 5:14). Yet there he stood, asserting that the best way to quench a teenage boy's sex drive was to expose him to as much sexually explicit photography as the young man wanted.

Half of today's sexually active teen males have their first sexual experience between ages 11 and 13. Yet, this elder believes that by letting his boys feed their sexual appetite at home, it will have less power over them when they are outside his control. How could anyone be so naive, unless his own experience has made these pictures seem tame? And that is just the point. We have grown accustomed to the sexual sin of our culture. The constant exposure has blinded us to its pervasiveness but not made us immune to its power.

The Erosion. Our increasing blindness to immorality proves how sinister is its erosive effect upon our standards. Some Christians today regularly partake of sexually explicit entertainments of the sort only the worst elements of our society would venture to see less than a generation ago. Only months ago I spoke to a campus ministry group on the need for the witness of holy lives to reach the university community. After I spoke, I learned the young people were going as a group to a local theater to watch the latest steamy, R-rated romance. I do not believe they were ignoring me or being rebellious. These were committed college students, courageous in their stand for Christ in many areas of campus life. Popular movies are simply so much a part of the entertainment experience of this generation that the group did not even question the vulgarities they were about to "enjoy" together.

Even in my seminary classroom, young men training for the ministry must be challenged to apply their theology of holiness to their entertainments. Sometimes it takes real convincing to persuade today's seminarians that a minister can hardly be an example of holiness if his illustrations indicate that he is a regular imbiber of sexually explicit entertainments—even if such references do show he is "culturally informed." God calls believers to purity, not to intimacy with popular culture. He desires holiness more from his leaders than articulateness with evil (Rom. 16:19; Eph. 5:3–4, 12).

Why is it so hard to see the obvious sexual sin around us and in us? The answer can only be that we have grown increasingly callous (Eph. 4:16). Most of my generation can remember when we had our first exposure to pornographic literature or sneaked in a theater to see our first dirty movie. How old were you? Probably in your early teens? Despite the years that have passed, we can remember that first searing exposure to gross evil because its nature is to etch itself on our minds and memories, there to keep doing its damage year after year. As corrosive as that experience is for a teenager, imagine the damage being done today to young children whose explicit sex education can begin even in preschool years. The ready accessibility of cable-TV and video recordings suggests that children no longer have to wait until their teens for their first secondhand sexual fix. They (and their parents) are bringing the sexual materials into their homes with the flip of a switch. What will the effects be of seeing such pornography at ages 3, 4, and 5 instead of ages 13, 14, and 15?

We are beginning to see the sad results already. For example, the current pop craze among teens, the media says, is horror-porn videos. Because there are few regulations on the rental of video tapes, teens can give parties at which the entertainment is violent, perverse sex films. Even before they are mature, young people are apparently needing more and more hard-core materials to satiate their sexual drives.

Callousness creates insensitivity and breeds monsters. When sexuality is seen as an experiential thrill rather than an expression of love, people are perceived as objects. Sex becomes selfish; love is equated to lust; and the very fabric of civilized society unravels. One of every four girls living today will be sexually assaulted in her lifetime—and one in every seven boys. When such unthinkable sin reaches such a magnitude, no element of society escapes unscathed. A year ago I spent a weekend at the home of a lawyer who heads the largest legal firm in a neighboring state. He says his firm's fastest-growing caseload involves civil suits of a very particular nature against churches. The suits allege child molestation in church day-care centers, day schools, and Sunday schools. When persons become objects, even the most innocent in the presumably safest of settings are vulnerable.

As sexual license becomes mass entertainment, people become possessions, love and passion become hopelessly confused. We date to gratify our longings and marry to satisfy self. Broken marriages and a generation of parentless children are the legacy of our national assent to sexual immorality. Young and old stumble from relationship to relationship looking for persistent pleasure, but the selfishness of the quest perpetually deprives them of real fulfillment. As jaded, self-absorbed individuals learn that you can never really satisfy lusts, you merely tire of persons, one in every two marriages fail. By the end of this decade, over half of the nation's children will no longer be living with both natural parents. We are a society at risk when we let our lusts determine our pleasures and therefore set our commitments and priorities.

When you begin to get even a glimpse of the degree to which immorality is warping and threatening our families, you may be angry, frightened, depressed, or totally overwhelmed! You may say, "What's the use of objecting? Why fight it? Immorality is too pervasive and too accepted. No one can do anything about it. The situation is hopeless." Such comments are why we still need Daniel's example. The Lord teaches us through Daniel what we are to do when sin seems invincible. What do we do? We do our duty.

The Stand. Yes, the sin seems overwhelming. Yes, its elimination is beyond our human abilities. But God says we must nevertheless continue doing our duty. Our commitment must echo Joshua, who said in a time of pervasive sin in his nation, ". . . as for me and my household, we will serve the LORD" (Josh. 24:15b). We must serve the Lord and let him take care of the rest. When we stand our ground, he will accomplish his good purpose through us, just as he used the duty of Daniel to triumph over evil. Our God has not changed; neither must our willing commitment to serve him dutifully.

On our family vacation last summer we visited the Great Sand Dunes National Park in Colorado. The dunes in this park are not ordinary sand piles. These shifting mountains climb as high as 900 feet and run for miles as a result of wind-driven sand being funneled through the great mountain pass. Round the dunes circles a river whose water is dispersed by the huge quantity of sand into so many rivulets that the entire river broadens and shallows out to wading depth. Even our children could walk across this river, and they loved this giant, fast-flowing wading pool. Our three-year-old, Jordan, particularly enjoyed standing firm in one of the rivulets against the current that threatened to bowl him over. It was laughable to watch—a child trying to hold back a river. Yet a minor miracle occurred whenever our son stood his ground firm enough, long enough. Then the sand in the current would begin to pile up against him, gathering at his feet and heaping up around his knees until eventually the river would go around him. When the child stood his ground, he triumphed over the river!

Our society's sinfulness can seem like a river that threatens to sweep away God's children in its flow. The river that threatens you might be a crisis of integrity or the pressures of professional compromise. The world says, "Give in. The stand you take will make no difference. Why get yourself hurt?" "Why fight the inevitable?" God says, "Dig in. Plant your feet firmly in my Word and let me triumph through you." If the problem is controlling your own passions, the world says, "Give up. There is no reason to deny yourself pleasure." God says, "Stand up. Be a beacon of holiness in a dark world where energy and happiness are exhausted on selfish eroticism." Wherever temptation confronts you, stand your ground. Carve a piece of the kingdom of God out of this world by claiming a corner of it for him. God triumphs in duty. Again and again, he calls you to duty.

The Faith of Duty

Duty cannot be separated from faith. Duty without faith is merely the product of dogged resolve, slavish fear, blind obedience, or simple stubbornness. The duty God requires is not so senseless. Faith makes duty reasonable, purposeful, and fulfilling.

Notice how the Scriptures record the direction Daniel prayed during his daily devotions—in "his upstairs room where the windows opened toward Jerusalem" (6:10). Why did Daniel direct his prayer to his people's holy city? Was Jerusalem like Mecca, in that you have to be facing the right direction for your prayers to work? Did God stay in Jerusalem? No, of course Daniel did not believe that his God, who had miraculously saved him time after time in Babylon, resided only in Jerusalem. Why, then, did Daniel focus on Jerusalem?

Remember, Daniel is a prophet. Following this final chapter of the prophet's life history are Daniel's amazing prophesies of the victories to come in Jerusalem. The captives from Judah will return to the holy city, Jerusalem, which will be restored. From its former ruins will rise a Savior who will defeat forever the enemy who "prowls around like a roaring lion looking for someone to devour" (1 Peter 5:8). As Daniel did his duty, his physical eyes could see only ruin, despair, and danger. But, through the eyes of faith, Daniel saw much more. By focusing on Jerusalem he saw sure victory, certain hope, and future triumph. Duty opened the windows of prayer, but faith empowered that duty with the vision of God's conquering purposes. The eyes of faith saw ruined Jerusalem shining again as the great symbol of God's abiding care and protection.

We, too, can do our duty without dumb resolve or hopeless fatalism if we fix our eyes of faith on the triumph that God is surely seeking through us. God is continually establishing his kingdom. He is a victorious, saving God who triumphs over evil through the loyalty of his faithful soldiers who stand their ground. He shut the mouths of the lions when Daniel was cast into their den. When we are held in the clutches of sin and Satan, God saves us, too. The lion of darkness could have mauled and scarred us all for an eternity, but God has rescued us. With the sacrificial triumph of his own Son, God shut the mouth of the raging lion Satan. Now, by faith, we see this God and can do our duty joyfully in the face of overwhelming sin and personal danger. Because we have seen God working on our behalf, we can do our duty and leave the consequences to God. We know his compassion and our faith sees his victory. We trust in the One who will silence the evil lion's roar forever.

Pastor Wyatt George of Murphysboro, Illinois, tells of an amazing Christmas card he recently received from retired missionary friends Vincent and Margaret Crossett. In the

1940s the Crossetts were missionaries in mainland China. They struggled against poverty and paganism in a remote village to tell others about Jesus. Although the work was slow and painstaking, after much sacrifice a small church (more like a simple Bible study) seemed almost established. But right on the threshold of this small triumph for the kingdom of God, Satan began his prowl. When the Communist Chinese government inaugurated the Cultural Revolution of 1948–9, all foreign missionaries were forced to leave the country.

How the Crossetts hated to leave. Their fledgling flock of believers hardly seemed ready to stand the coming onslaught. An atheistic, dictatorial government dedicated to wiping out all Christian influence began its rule with ruthless power. How could the little church survive? From a worldly perspective there was nothing anyone could do. The church appeared destined for extinction. But Vincent and Margaret do not see as the world sees. They saw no reason to despair because, through eyes of faith, they saw a God who is faithful to those who honor him.

The Crossetts continued to do their duty. Yes, the political wall of China went up, and the missionaries were closed out—but not their prayers. For nearly forty years the Crossetts daily kept their prayer windows opened toward China. They did their duty in the faith that God could triumph though an institution of sin had swept the land like a mighty river. The Crossetts heard nothing of their Chinese friends for four decades, but still they dutifully prayed for God to be victorious in the church they left behind.

Finally, the wall came down again. As the political climate changed, this ancient eastern land again opened to the West. The Crossetts returned and hastened to the village where they had left the tiny struggling group of believers. There was no "small church" in the village anymore! Instead, from that Bible study had grown a church of four thousand people. This body of believers had spawned other churches. In the surrounding region had sprung up nearly a dozen churches, each with a membership of no less than a thousand people. All the Crossetts did was pray. It was all they *could* do. But through their faith and duty God triumphed. He turned back the flood of evil. He shut the lions' mouths again. The God of Daniel is alive and well. The victories of God are as close as faith and duty.

Christian, what are you facing today? Is the sin around you or in you so great that you cannot see the sense of fighting it? Stand your ground. Do what is right and let God take care of the rest. He can and he will. There may be so much wrong, so much upheaval and confusion, that you wonder what to do. And, even if you know what to do, you may wonder what's the use. You think nothing could change your boss, or your marriage, or your circumstances. Things may appear to be such a mess that there seems no chance of ever straightening them out. But, however confusing the circumstances, however obscure may seem solutions in the dirt and clutter of your situation, God still explains clearly what he expects.

We cry out in anguish, "What do you want from me, God? Surely you have some new answers for this mess. Tell me what you want me to do."

God answers. Listen carefully. He is speaking now, softly and gently: *Whisk-Whisk.*

No matter what the trial, God asks you to listen to the sound of a broom, a broom held by a servant named Daniel. That broom is sweeping away all the clutter of our situations and the confusion of our questions. Do you hear it? The broom whispers: *Whisk-Whisk.* God calls: "Faith and duty. Faith and duty. Do what I command and trust me to take care of the rest." God does not ask you to solve the problem. He simply asks you—as he asked Daniel—to sweep clean the path to his purpose. *Whisk-Whisk.* His Word echoes, "Faith and duty." His promise rings: "Triumph and victory."

"This is what I ask of you, Christian," says the Lord God Almighty. "Stand your ground."